# REDEEMED

## GRACE TO LIVE EVERY DAY
## BETTER THAN BEFORE

LifeWay Press®
Nashville, Tennessee

Published by LifeWay Press® • © 2016 Angela Thomas-Pharr

ISBN 9781430051565 • Item 005772641

Dewey decimal classification: 248.84

Subject headings: DISCIPLESHIP \ CHRISTIAN LIFE \ SALVATION

To order additional copies of this resource, write to LifeWay Church Resources Customer Service; One LifeWay Plaza; Nashville, TN 37234-0113; order online at *www.lifeway.com;* fax 615.251.5933; phone toll free 800.458.2772; email *orderentry@lifeway.com;* or visit the LifeWay Christian Store serving you.

*Printed in the United States of America*

Adult Ministry Publishing • LifeWay Church Resources

One LifeWay Plaza • Nashville, TN 37234-0152

# CONTENTS

# INTRODUCTION

Hello dear friends,

A couple of years ago, my son, Grayson, spent the summer serving alongside a ministry in South America. Sometime before he left, our family was having a pretty typical kitchen-counter discussion. I'm sure there was some random philosophical question, with a little science, math, theology, and some mama-Bible-quoting thrown in.

I have no idea where our discussion was headed that day, but I think it was something about differing perspectives on Christian worldview. After a while, Grayson said he looked forward to discussing similar things with the people he would be serving in South America. From the little I knew about where he was going, I didn't think he was going to meet many people anxious to discuss worldviews. I told him, "Baby, I hate to disappoint you, but I don't think most of the people you're going to meet will give a rip about any of this. They have a heart problem caused by a sin problem. They just want to be happy and have no idea why they're miserable or lonely or scared, or why they keep living they way they do. God is sending you to tell them Jesus is the answer. His forgiveness is the way. They need to know the very real, very present love of God to redeem their lives. They need the most important thing!"

That's kind of how I feel about this study. We could spend our time working through a hundred different redemption details, but knowing more about being redeemed is not the most important thing. The actual, ongoing transformation of a life being redeemed by God is the most important thing.

So here's what this study is about and what I hope you gain:

> Your life being redeemed and continuing to be redeemed until you are home with God in heaven
>
> A biblical understanding of what it means to be redeemed
>
> The ability to explain being redeemed to someone who doesn't know God, and the confidence to invite them to be redeemed because of what He has done for you
>
> A beautiful, grace-filled walk with Jesus Christ
>
> A group of friends who are being redeemed alongside you.

That's exactly why we've changed up the format with this study. I'm trying to do everything I can with words on a page, to connect your very real, everyday life with the very, real presence and power of God. Here's all I know: When those two things intersect, lives are going to change. Healing will happen. Prayers will be answered. You will know God even more intimately as your Redeemer. Your life will give evidence of being redeemed. And you will tell others what God has done.

Last year, our family committed to 40 days of prayer. Our 40 days wasn't anything fancy or hard, just an individual commitment to be intentional about praying every single day. We began with empty prayer journals and asked God what He wanted us to pray about in those days.

Because our family's 40 days were so profound and powerful, and because a 6-week Bible study has 42 days from start to finish, this study includes 40 days of prayer. In addition to praying each day, I'm also hoping you'll join us in reading through the Book of Psalms and meditating on the verses. Check out "40 Days: The Psalms, Meditation, and Prayer" on page 188 for more info.

I am praying this is not a sweet, little sugar-coated Bible study. I'm praying for fire. *Lord God, set our hearts ablaze!* I'm praying for God's great redemption truth to collide head-on and full-force with your greatest need. If God does what I believe He wants to do, some things in your life and mine are getting ready to change for good. Being changed for good doesn't mean every step along the way will be easy, or that every truth will make you feel warm and fuzzy. But God has made a covenant with us that a life being redeemed is the better life. May we long for God's better. May these weeks become a life-changing encounter with God. And when this book is finished, I hope God has begun something inside your soul that doesn't end. You want to keep reading His Word. You want to keep praying in His presence. You want to keep being redeemed.

If I were sitting across from you right now, I'd lean in and say,

*My new friend, you are truly known and precious to God. Please don't be afraid or intimated by His holy love. God did not bring you to this study to condemn you. He brought you here to speak to you and to help you. God made each one of us creative, unique, beautiful, and interesting. And by His grace, you and I can still become all our Father dreamed we will be:*

An authentic woman who bears His image

One who is kind-hearted and confident, not passive or fragile

An influencer who leads without pretense or manipulation

A dreamer who runs toward her dreams without striving

Doing the work that helps us grow, yet living in contentment along the way

Intentionally making art with the life we've been given

Becoming wise and peaceful

Loving and gentle

Humble in heart

Grateful

Redeemed.

Welcome to *Redeemed*.

With love and gratefulness,

*Angela Thomas-Pharr*

www.angelathomaspharr.com

# WHEN LOVE MAKES A PROMISE

# I CAN'T

Hello, my friend.

Sometimes, when a person wants something to change, she'll think about it, talk about it, read about it, cry about it, and pray about it. They might journal about it. Download an app about it. Make a list about it. Go see a counselor about it. Sign up for a class about it. Put reminder notes on the mirror about it. Find an accountability group about it. Graph a chart about it. Beat themselves up about it.

And then one day, they just forget about it.

Until they think about it again. And the string is pulled that spins the crazy-maker top into circles all over again. Only the next time, it's always faster.

The Lord knows we have all tried to change some things about ourselves. We've tried to help other people change their lives. We've even jumped in to help change the world. A lot of us have tried and tried, with very little real change to show for all these circles. And now, most everybody I know is tired.

Maybe you know this. When you are tired and your spirit is heavy, the heart begins to mumble the saddest word: *Whatever*.

I may not know many things, but spinning in circles, weariness, and mumbling—I could teach a master class in those. You see, I have longed for spiritual and emotional maturity; to improve myself and my habits; to have greater discipline; for quick obedience when the Holy Spirit leads; to be a woman ever-increasing in wisdom, patience, and grace, who inwardly and outwardly is being changed and redeemed.

And the truth is God has moved powerfully in my life. But mercy, I could sit down and cry over all the times I abandoned His power, having taken two steps forward and then turned around to run half a mile back. Too many years have been wasted spinning in circles, going nowhere.

*Maybe you know something about spinning in circles too. How would you fill in this blank?*

*I've given up trying* _____.

See if you can relate to this:

> For I do not understand my own actions. For I do not do what I want,
> but I do the very thing I hate. . . . For I have the desire to do what
> is right, but not the ability to carry it out. For I do not do the good
> I want, but the evil I do not want is what I keep on doing.
> **ROMANS 7:15,18b-19**

Can I tell you how it humbles me to open my Bible and read those words? We rarely encounter that kind of vulnerability, and, yet, the apostle Paul recounted with such transparency his own inability to change. Then, in verse 24, we can feel the agony and downright hopelessness in his words.

> Wretched man that I am! Who will deliver me from this body of death?
> **ROMANS 7:24**

I don't know how you arrived at this study. I don't know anything about your life so far, but I imagine if the truth were told, somewhere inside, a part of you is asking, maybe even crying, "Who will deliver me?"

*Who will deliver me from my pain? My regret? My habits? My choices? My secrets? My sin?*

*Who will deliver me from these crazy circles? And the wasted time? And the weariness? And the loneliness?*

*Who will deliver me from . . . whatever?*

Okay, were some of those questions a little deeper than you were ready to go? Like, it's the first day of a new Bible study, and you were just gonna practice sitting down with all your stuff and warming up to the whole idea of whatever this *Redeemed* is going to be.

Honestly, I've been worried about jumping in too fast. I want you to know your heart is safe here in this study. You will never turn one of these pages and get a spiritual-shaming from me. I will never set you up to be emotionally manipulated.

I want to earn your trust, mainly because I want you to give these weeks more than just your time. I want you to go all in. Wholeheartedly and devoted. Not to me, but to God's truth. Maybe you're already feeling like you're here for a reason, even if you haven't had time to think about it yet. For all those reasons we don't yet know, the Holy Spirit would not let me dilly-dally with your heart today, put us on a slow train, or help you spin more circles going nowhere.

Here's is my goal for us: When you and I finish the last day of this book, not only will we know our Redeemer and His plan called redemption, we will be experiencing His very real and substantial redemption in our own lives. We will be redeemed. And our lives, character, relationships, and callings will continue being redeemed.

I didn't come to play. Not with God's truth, nor with your heart. So would you picture me standing beside you—with the truth of all my insecurities, struggles, and flaws—wholeheartedly and honestly asking, *Who will deliver us from ourselves? Who will stop us from staying the same? Who will keep us from becoming modern-day scoffers? I am complacent. And inconsistent. And unworthy. I am all things I don't want to be. Who will deliver me?*

The apostle Paul's soul released its desperate cry, "Who will deliver me?" and immediately, I mean, very-next-sentence immediately, his heart knew the answer.

> Thanks be to God through Jesus Christ our Lord!
> **ROMANS 7:25**

You are I are doing this study together because we both need to be delivered from ourselves. Even with our diversity of cultures and opinions, I bet we could agree on a couple of things. We both want to become the best possible version of who we were created to be. And we both want to live the best possible version of the life we've been given

In A.D. 495, Augustine wrote that most people just want a happy life.[1] Nothing about the human spirit has changed. But here's the thing: The deep ruts I've made spinning circles serve no purpose except to prove that the life I long to live and the woman I long to become will not be created by my own hands. I can't. I can't make the life or the person I dream of being happen. I've tried. Lord knows I've tried. I desperately need someone to come and rescue me. I need someone to shape me, reshape me, lead me, walk with me, and take me the rest of the way home.

As I just typed those words, that old heavy feeling of discouragement wanted to come in and sit with me like it's done so many times before. But there was no room beside me today because, like Paul, I remembered the most glorious truth: *Thanks be to God through Jesus Christ our Lord.* We have a Redeemer, and we shall be redeemed.

Would you open your Bible and start reading Romans 7:15 until the end of the chapter? Paul took a little inventory of his great need. Are you ready to start this thing strong? And vulnerable? And honest?

What about your great need? Finish this question for God with some of your own personal needs.

*Who will deliver me from* _____?

Wait! Don't close your Bible yet. Paul isn't finished with us. Find Romans 8:1, and fill in the blanks below,

There is therefore now _____ _____
for _____ who are in Christ Jesus.
**ROMANS 8:1**

Do you see the beauty of what just happened? Romans 7 reads like someone shouting, "I can't!"

You have to believe the very minute Paul wrote those vulnerable words of confession, the heaviness of old despair wanted to hold him down and keep shaming him. But, bless God, Paul did not go down that day. He remembered, "Jesus Christ, our Lord, is my Deliverer! I belong to Jesus now. This struggle cannot keep shaming me. Jesus took my condemnation to the cross. And there is therefore now no condemnation for me."

No matter your struggles. No matter your failures. No matter how stinking awful your track record, if you belong to Jesus Christ, "there is therefore now no condemnation."

## PREPARING FOR 40 DAYS

Sometimes we believe we can't because we never have. Maybe you've never had the time to be intentional about reading through an entire book of the Bible, thinking about what God is saying to you, and then spending consistent time in a conversation with Him, called prayer. It's okay if your first thought about all this is, *I can't.*

In today's study, as I began to confess, *I can't,* to God, it was like a flood-gate opened, and all my *I can'ts* came pouring out. Where are you feeling the stress of *I can't* in your life today? Turn those into prayer. Let the gates of your heart swing open. God wants to come in.

*Oh God, I can't . . .*

# GOD CAN

If your life is like most, one of the first things you're feeling is, *I just can't do this study right now.* Here are some reasons you may feel like you can't continue:

- The timing is probably crummy.

- You are not physically or emotionally rested. Actually, you may find yourself smack dab in the middle of the most exhausting season of your life.

- You're in this alone. Not one friend has signed up to do this. No one in your family is on board. You just don't have any support.

- You're just not feeling it. Whatever "redeemed" is, it doesn't sound very exciting. You want to feel more excited.

- There are a lot of extra things going on in your life right now. And the kids, they're so busy.

   *Maybe I missed something, so help me out. List two more reasons why you can't commit to the next 40 days.*

So there you go. My five, plus your two. You should have a pretty strong list of reasons to close the book. Now you have it all down in black and white: *you can't.*

Can I tell you something?

- The timing will never get better. Not when you finish school. Not when you're married. Not when the kids are grown. Not when you retire. Never.

- You could wait until you're rested, but how long has it been since that last happened?

- The people who truly love you may never be able to support you in the ways you long to be supported. How many more years will that keep you from beginning?

- Feeling excited about something is rarely a good measure of value. I would love for you to feel excited. I actually believe those feelings may show up in the weeks to come, but then again, maybe not.

- Everything in the world that can fall on your head to distract you has probably already started falling. If it's any consolation to you, everything is falling here too.

Here's why I'm walking us through all of this. I desperately want us to begin this study in truth—to take an honest inventory of our hearts; the very real, everyday lives we lead; and the condition of our souls. If God has planned to show up in your life with the power to redeem, the first thing I am expecting you to face is resistance. We are not wackado people, so rest assured, any resistance you face will be rational, logical stuff. There will be 100 good reasons for you not to make this commitment right now.

*Let's press in a little further. Would you close your eyes for just a few minutes? As you do, will you think about one thing you know you cannot do? That's right. Something in your life you're giving up on. One thing you are sure you cannot do. We're not in a hurry, so don't skip this. Sit as long as you need, until you have it.*

Do you need God? Are you ready to search for Him? And fight against resistance to get to Him? If it's possible to fall in love with God, do you want to really love Him? If a woman can be changed by His power, do you need to be changed? If God can be your friend, do you want Him to be yours? Are you ready to hear God say, *Oh baby girl, I know you can't. But I can.*

God can.

Earlier we said every one of us needs a deliverer. Like Paul in Romans 7, our weary souls shout to the world, *I CAN'T. I can't do the very thing I want to do. And try to do. And dream of doing.* What I want you to know today is that the God of glory knows your great need, and He has already left heaven to help you.

*You.*

God left heaven to save you, to heal you, and to redeem you. He knows your struggles, your vulnerabilities, and your pain. He sees how you keep spinning in circles, revisiting the same places, disappointing the same people, listening to the same lies. The old patterns. The insecurities. The stupid habits. The addictions. All the ways you keep proving you can't improve, and you can't get unstuck. He knows you cannot change yourself.

And that has always been the point. You can't.

But God can.

You and I are not the first people to declare, *I can't*. Long before us, there was a Red Sea and the walls of Jericho and a lion's den and a stone rolled in front of a grave. And the people who needed God surely cried to heaven, *I can't*.

Here is the sweet mercy: The God of heaven hears when we cry, *I can't*. And even more amazing to me, He answers. The Bible says the love and mercy of God toward us never changes, so that when a desperate woman calls to Him, God stoops to her, moves closer to her, and answers her.

> Then you shall call, and the LORD will answer;
> you shall cry, and he will say, "Here I am."
> **ISAIAH 58:9**

Every time we say, *I can't*, the Bible has already declared, *God can*.

I believe God wants to begin responding to you this very day. We're not waiting until Week 5 to get closer to Him. Do you need God today? Then tell Him. Really take the time to tell Him. Bow your head now, or write your prayer out, but go ahead and tell Him that you need Him.

> *Maybe you long to finally believe God is real. Tell Him.*
> *Maybe you want to feel His presence with you. Ask Him.*
> *Maybe you want a better relationship with Him. Say that.*

Being redeemed is about being changed. No one can be redeemed in their own strength or by their own actions. If we are going to live as redeemed women with lives that keep being redeemed, there is only one answer. Each one of us needs a Redeemer.

We can't. Oh mercy, we really and truly can't. But hallelujah and praise be to God, He is our Redeemer, and He can.

Why does God want you to know He can be your Redeemer? Because He loves you.

He. Loves. You.

**How close is God to you right now? Here's what the Bible says:**

The LORD your God is with you wherever you go.
**JOSHUA 1:9**

Even though I walk through the valley of the shadow of death, I will fear no evil, for you are with me.
**PSALM 23:4**

The LORD is near to all who call on him.
**PSALM 145:18**

The Lord your God is in your midst, a mighty one who will save.
**ZEPHANIAH 3:17**

Behold, I am with you always, to the end of the age.
**MATTHEW 28:20b**

He has said, "I will never leave you nor forsake you."
**HEBREWS 13:5**

The theology of God's love and redemption is a really big deal, and I can't wait for us to know more about it. But for today, here's where we need to land:

When MY GREAT NEED accepts GOD'S GREAT LOVE, **REDEMPTION BEGINS.**
I CAN'T.                HE CAN.

God did not design us to spin in circles, staying the same, only more frustrated and discouraged with every passing year. We were made to grow and change. God's power to redeem—and keep redeeming—our lives is the means by which we are meant to grow and mature. You can try to dig down to find your bootstraps all you want, but God has so much more in mind for you and me.

Are you ready for God to do greater things in your life? Are you ready for redemption? Will you make a wholehearted commitment to our next 40 days together?

## PREPARING FOR 40 DAYS

Tomorrow we begin our 40 days of intentional time with God. If that sounds a little intimidating, let me put your mind at ease: There aren't any hard-and-fast rules about this. We all just need a little nudge sometimes. In the next 40 days, I'm hoping some of us begin spending consistent time with God, some recover the intimacy we used to have, and all of us find our time with the Lord sweeter than we've ever known.

Here's the goal: We're gonna read through the Book of Psalms and pray for the next 40 days. In a row. Even when you don't feel like it. And yes, I'm thankful to report, there is grace for puny, whiny-baby praying.

Here's what I'm expecting when we're through: you will never want to be away from God's Word or time with Him in prayer again.

DAY 1

# BEGINNING WITH PRAYER

Welcome to our first day of prayer. Day 1. Launch day. Go day. We're rollin' day.

*One of these days* is finally today.

I've been so excited about adding 40 days of prayer to this Bible study, I could burst. And then, at the very same time, I've been kind of nervous. Nervous because, *What if I'm wrong about adding this? What if people don't want to pray for 40 days? What if doing a Bible study and praying for 40 days is too confusing? Or too much? Or too hard? What if this becomes the smallest attended Bible study ever?* You know, I'm just over here in my house trying to go where God leads. I haven't taken a poll or anything. Actually, I haven't even asked anybody if they think I should add 40 days of prayer. I'm afraid they'll smile politely. So, with zero guarantees, I'm just going for it. We're praying for 40 days. Boom.

That declaration just sent me to my knees.

And it forces me to trust the Holy Spirit. You see, I can jump up and down, type in ALL CAPS, make teaching videos, post personal messages, write blog posts, and engage social media until we're all sick of me, but I cannot make one person engage her heart. I am forced to trust God because I can't get in my car and come over there and make you pray. I'm not assured anything I say or write in these pages will move your heart toward prayer. Maybe you signed up to watch some videos and fill in some blanks in this book, but this prayer thing? You're not sure. It might be too much to ask.

Here's why this matters so much.

A Bible study about being redeemed is awesome! We are going to learn some stuff! Big stuff! Smart, Bible-girl stuff! But here's what grabbed a hold of my heart and won't let go. What if this happens? What if you are doing the *Redeemed* study, and your life starts *being redeemed?*

Boom.

**40 DAYS OF PRAYER STARTS NOW!**

*I can't do that.* You already know you can't do that. But God can. As a matter of fact, He's been waiting for you to be here.

Prayer puts us in the presence of God. Entering into a conversation with God. Listening to God. Responding to God. Prayer is the link between having head knowledge about God and the soul that experiences the reality of God. In this study, prayer will be the difference-maker for all of us. The next 40 days will either be the time we learned some more "stuff" about God, or they will be the days we personally experienced the presence and power of God in our very souls.

I want us to get everything we can get while we're here. And if God allows, these days will only be the beginning for all of us. I can't make you pray, so I'm just praying that you'll pray. I'm inviting you to pray, but mostly, I'm trusting God, the only One with the power to persuade you.

## BEING REDEEMED

What in the world does *being redeemed* mean? *Redeemed* is one powerful word, but *being redeemed* is not just one thing in the Bible. There's a lot more explaining to do, but for the sake of beginning with the basic Bible truth, being redeemed involves three distinct parts of the Christian life:

> The moment you believe Jesus died to save you,
> *You are redeemed.*
> As you live the rest of your life growing as a follower of Christ,
> *You are being redeemed.*
> When you die and go to heaven,
> *You will be fully and finally redeemed.*

A lot of theology and some technical words are involved, but ultimately, *being redeemed* is about *being changed.* When you first believe in Jesus, also known as the day of your **salvation,** *you are redeemed.* On that day, the Bible says your standing with God is immediately changed, you are given a new identity, and the Holy Spirit comes to live in your soul. A Christ-follower (a Christian) is changed from death to life, dark to light, lost to found. You go from a stranger to God—to a daughter of the Most High King.

> *Based on what you already know, list some of the immediate things that change when someone places his or her faith in Jesus.*

From the day of believing until we arrive in heaven, you and I live the Christian life with a new ambition—to be conformed to the image of Christ. The process of the old woman I have been, being changed into the likeness of Christ, is the ongoing work of *being redeemed.* This process is also known in the Bible as **sanctification.**

> For those He foreknew He also predestined to be conformed to the image of His Son.
> **ROMANS 8:29 (HCSB)**

> And we all, with unveiled face, beholding the glory of the Lord, are being transformed into the same image from one degree of glory to another. For this comes from the Lord who is the Spirit.
> **2 CORINTHIANS 3:18**

> *How have you seen someone being changed as they continued to follow Jesus? (Maybe that person was you.) List a few examples.*

And then one day, hallelujah, the journey to heaven will be over. Upon a believer's death, she is immediately taken into the presence of God, where she is *finally and fully redeemed.* That means being fully remade into the image of Christ. Fully in the presence of the Lord. This eternal change is called **glorification.**

> But our citizenship is in heaven, and from it we await a Savior, the Lord Jesus Christ, who will transform our lowly body to be like his glorious body, by the power that enables him even to subject all things to himself.
> **PHILIPPIANS 3:20-21**

There are three unique phases in our redemption, and each phase of being redeemed involves being changed:

**SALVATION:** We are *changed* from unbeliever to believer.

**SANCTIFICATION:** We continue *being changed* into the image of Christ.

**GLORIFICATION:** We are *eternally changed* into the likeness of Christ.

Since you are still reading these words on earth, at this very moment, you can only be one of two places. On your life time line, you are either pre-salvation or post-salvation. Either you do not believe in Jesus or you believe. You are either unredeemed or redeemed. And in case you are wondering, God never uses vague words like *sorta* or *kind of* to describe our position before Him. The redeemed have made a certain decision; the unredeemed have not.

This Bible study is about two things:

1. **MAKING A REDEEMED DECISION**—being changed into a follower of Jesus Christ.
2. **MAKING A REDEEMED JOURNEY**—being changed into His image.

It's about becoming *the* redeemed, who are being redeemed constantly. And both of these things require you to choose. God will provide the power for both, but the choice is always and only yours. In just the same way, prayer is how we connect our lives to God's power, but praying is also your choice. You can choose not to. But I'm praying something specific is stirring inside of you right this moment, a flicker of hope in your soul. Will you give hope 40 days? 40 real, honest days? Will you commit to 40 days of prayer? Let's mark it down with the dates and your signed pledge:

*Today, _____, I am beginning 40 days of*

*prayer. The date of the 40th day will be: _____.*

*I long to be redeemed.*

*Sincerely committed, _____*

# READ AND MEDITATE

Today, we'll begin reading and meditating through the Book of Psalms. In the back of this book, you can check out "40 Days: The Psalms, Meditation, and Prayer" on page 188.

As you turn from today's study toward a time in prayer, read the first two chapters in the Book of Psalms and spend a few moments meditating on the words God is using to speak to you today.

## MY DAY 1 PRAYER FOR YOU

*Oh Father, our God and our Redeemer, may Your presence fill the place where my friend sits with Your Word. Give her a fresh, new awareness of You. Give her the gift of knowing and believing You are near. Cover her with Your grace. Convince her that she is loved and welcomed into Your presence. In Jesus' precious name, amen.*

# RESPOND IN PRAYER

Here we go . . . praying for 40 days together.

**Some words to help you begin:**

- *Father, You are . . .*

- *Father, forgive me . . .*

- *Father, redeem me . . .*

- *Father, be near to me . . .*

- *Father, be glorified in me . . .*

_____

_____

_____

_____

_____

_____

_____

_____

_____

_____

_____

_____

_____

_____

_____

_____

_____

_____

_____

DAY 2

# BEGINNING WITH A WORD

So, this is how this whole thing started.

One morning I said to my husband, Scott, "I have no idea when I'm supposed to write the next Bible study, but I think God spoke the title to me in my sleep." Here's the part where you should know that I rarely dream. Lots of people seem to have very detailed dreams, but not me. I'm one of those go-to-sleep-and-wake-up kind of people. You can imagine the she's-never-said-that-before look in Scott's eyes when he asked, "What's the title?"

"Redeemed," is all I said—because it's all I knew.

**Redeemed: points to something that has been recovered by paying a sum to get it back.[3]**

Well, right then, my big lug of a hunky husband started crying. Then I started crying. And somehow, through all those choked up tears, Scott forced two words,

"That's it," he said through his tears.

This project began the morning God whispered, *Redeemed.* And ever since then, I've been trying to pay attention. Looking, reading, searching, listening, asking, seeking. My first inclination was to reach for the deep theologians with their weighty thoughts and academic words, so I did. I jumped into the study of redemption like it was the first day of summer, and I was the neighborhood kid sprinting all the way to the pool for a running-jump cannonball into the deep end. So. very. excited.

I guess I spent six months or more in a full-fledged redemption theology geek-out. I loved studying so much, I considered going back to seminary to get my doctorate or traveling to international libraries to find better, geekier books. The deeper I dove, the more there was to find. Complex theologies with intricate biblical patterns, all woven together with fine threads of differing perspective, opinion, and insight. Honestly, I loved all of my time down there in the deep end, swimming around on the bottom, discovering new thought trinkets to handle and examine.

But there is one very important thing to remember about being in over your head at the deep end of the pool. There is no air down there. Nada. And no air means no life. Maybe you know what I mean.

Have you ever felt in over your head with God? Maybe you try to pay attention at church, but the teaching doesn't connect with your head, much less your heart. Do parts of the Bible ever feel like thick patches of God-fog to you? You want to seek God. You want to know Him. But you can't ever seem to find your way.

*Take a minute and jot down some of the ways you have felt in over your spiritual head in the past. Understanding the Bible? Theology? Other religions? Be as specific as you can.*

*How would you describe knowing God right now? Is it:*

☐ *He's becoming more clear. I'm learning to trust Him and see where God wants me to go!*
☐ *I'm in a God fog. I truly want a real relationship, but I can't seem to find my way.*
☐ *I have no idea what you're talking about. Is this a Bible study? I thought I signed up for a book club.*

*While we're taking a look inside, what about your soul today?*

☐ *Filled with meaning and purpose for my life.*
☐ *Being healed.*
☐ *Wounded. Hurting. Lonely.*
☐ *Empty and bored, or empty and distressed.*

Do you remember yesterday's lesson? You and I begin a relationship with God when we are redeemed. As we continue being redeemed, the relationship grows deeper and sweeter as we are being changed into the likeness of Christ.

Your relationship with God is not meant to be a scary dive into murky waters, but a real, thriving, everyday relationship. Being redeemed helps us live a better life with meaning and purpose! God's grace removes our shame. He meets us right where we are. And His love can remove our fear.

Our earth assignment is to keep being redeemed. Yep, our everyday life, in this crazy world, during these crazy days.

**Dear God, I cannot love Thee the way I want to. You are the slim crescent of a moon that I see and my self is the earth's shadow that keeps me from seeing all the moon . . . what I am afraid of, dear God, is that my self shadow will grow so large that it blocks the whole moon, and that I will judge myself by the shadow that is nothing. I do not know You God because I am in the way.[4]**
**FLANNERY O'CONNOR**

And, as you well know, in the real world, somebody's gotta climb out of the deep end of the pool and make dinner, pay the bills, and mow the lawn. That's you and me—and all those who choose to follow Jesus Christ.

In the weeks ahead, we may do a few cannonballs into deeper theology from time to time, but I want you to know we're going to keep our heads above water. We're going to breathe the fresh air of God's truth and grace. Being redeemed is one of the most important concepts in the Bible, and these weeks are going to make a real difference in your life.

We're going to be redeemed.

If you've ever helped a child with algebra, you might remember that solving an equation begins by reducing the equation to its simplest form. One of God's sweet gifts of grace is that big, complex theology, like being redeemed, becomes even more glorious when reduced to it's simplest form. My apologetics professor taught us to approach the Bible like this.[5]

**The main things are the plain things, and the plain things are the main things.**

The un-plain things and the un-main things may be interesting, but the most important things in the Bible are the plain, main things. Hallelujah and amen. So, with that clear guide in mind, if we could choose one word to communicate the message of the entire Bible, then that plain, main word might be:

**If you prefer theological cannonballs over slow-wading, read *Redemption Accomplished and Applied*, by John Murray, Scottish professor of systematic theology.**

*Redeemed.*

Or, we could also choose an equally wonderful plain, main word like:

*Loved.*

And, if we had to choose only one verse to represent the whole Bible, that plain, main verse might be:

For God so loved the world, that he gave his only Son, that whoever believes in him should not perish but have eternal life.
JOHN 3:16

*Circle the verbs in the previous verse. Now use those verbs to help you list three main, plain truths the verse teaches us.*

*1.*

*2.*

*3.*

*Now, write your name in all the blanks below. This is what it means for you to be redeemed:*

*For God so loved _____, that he gave his only Son, that if _____ believes in him _____ will not perish but _____ will have eternal life.*

**JOHN 3:16**

Here is a plain, main truth from the Bible: You are loved by God. So very, very loved. Because God loves you, He wants to help you, and He doesn't want to wait for some far away time to become part of your life. He sent His Son long ago because He wants to help you today.

# READ AND MEDITATE

*TODAY'S READING: PSALMS 3–4*

**MY DAY 2 PRAYER FOR YOU**

*O Father, You are glorious, and Your Word is truly our help and our path. Will You give us two things today—the sweet clarity that comes from simple truth and the deep hunger to know You more? Lord, will You continue to make Your presence known in the places where we pray. Father, hear our stumbles and mumbles. Help us know how to begin. Welcome each one into Your presence with a joy that floods her heart with grace. In the name of Jesus, amen and amen.*

# RESPOND IN PRAYER

[He] prayed continually to God.
**ACTS 10:2**

As an instinct, prayer is a response to our innate but fragmentary knowledge of God . . . As a gift of the Spirit, however, prayer becomes the continuation of a conversation God has started. If that conversation proceeds, as in the best conversations, praying becomes meeting with God—heaven in the ordinary.[6]
**TIMOTHY KELLER**

**DAY 3**

# BEGINNING WITH A PROMISE

My mind cannot comprehend the great time line of eternity, but the Bible tells us, from eternity past, long before we ever were, God already loved each one of us with a perfect and unwavering love.

> I have loved you with an everlasting love.
> **JEREMIAH 31:3b**

> He chose us in him before the foundation of the world.
> **EPHESIANS 1:4**

The Bible declares you and I, and all human beings, were created from God's love, for His love, to enjoy His love.

> We have come to know and to believe the love that God has for us. God is love.
> **1 JOHN 4:16**

In your Bible, turn to the Book of Genesis. As you read verses 1-25 of the first chapter, they unfold with ever-increasing brilliance, outlining the order of God's perfect creation. Beginning in verse 11 and continuing through verse 25, God used a specific phrase to define the way He created those groups. Find that phrase and fill in the word below:

*God created each _____ according to their/its _____.*

Vegetation, trees, creatures, livestock. Over and over, God is exacting when He says every living thing made so far was made according to their *kind*. And now, we arrive at the pinnacle of creation.

*From verse 26, fill in the blanks below:*

*Then God said, "Let us make man in our _____, after our*
*_____."*

*And verse 27:*

*So God _____ man in _____ own*
*_____, in the image of God he created _____;*
*male and _____ he created _____.*

**Being made in the image of God means:**

Do you see what just happened? Unlike all the previous creation, God created man in His own image.

**• Man is like God.**

**• Man represents God.**

Every single human being—no matter his or her race, age, disability, weakness or sin—equally bears the status of being in God's image.

*How should we value and respect the image-bearing of all human beings?*

*With our conduct:*

*By giving honor:*

*By providing protection:*

And the Lord God planted a garden in Eden, in the east,
and there he put the man whom he had formed.
**GENESIS 2:8**

In the garden of Eden, Adam and Eve enjoyed all the gifts of the perfect creation:

1. They ruled and subdued the earth (1:28).
2. They were made perfectly for one another (2:18-23).
3. They enjoyed a perfect relationship with one another and with God (2:25).
4. The were blessed by God (1:28).
5. They were morally perfect like the image of God and given the free will to reason and choose (1:27).

In this first scene of humanity, there was only perfect creation and perfect relationship in the garden of Eden. Nothing needed to be redeemed. Nothing was lost nor needed to be found. Nothing was enslaved nor needed to be set free.

But even from eternity past, God knew His beloved creation would choose to disobey Him. In the garden of Eden, Adam and Eve chose one willful act of disobedience. With their choice, came consequences. Look at Genesis 3:23-24, some of the saddest verses in the Bible.[7]

> Therefore the LORD God sent him out from the garden of Eden to work the ground from which he was taken. He drove out the man, and at the east of the garden of Eden he placed the cherubim and a flaming sword that turned every way to guard the way to the tree of life.
> **GENESIS 3:23-24**

The NIV Bible translation says God "banished" them from the garden. Then, to assure their permanent exile, He stationed a cherubim with a flaming sword to guard the entrance to the garden. Adam and Eve's perfect relationship with God was forever changed. Can you picture this sad Scene Two? Adam and Eve are walking away from the only life they've ever known—perfection. The garden and its beauty is behind them. A cherubim wielding a flaming sword is on guard. Only the desolate, cursed land is in front of them.

The day of Adam and Eve's disobedience is known as "the fall" because all creation fell from the grace of God. Adam was the divinely-appointed representative of the human race, and when Adam chose disobedience, the entire human race fell with him. All of creation, including humanity, suffered the consequences of the fall:

- Man was separated from the presence of God and could only experience Him from a distance.
- Life without pain or death was lost and the certainty of pain and death came to all creation.
- Man's innocent nature in the garden was replaced by a sinful nature, walking among evil and darkness.
- Perfect relationship turned to shame. Nothing would ever be the same.

**Why would a perfect God create a being that may not choose to love Him?**

**God is love. He is both the true reality and the true feeling of love. He did not create us like puppets to be pulled by strings. Being forced to love anyone is no love at all. God created humans with the ability to choose or to reject His love, so that He would be glorified by real love.**

One trespass led to condemnation for all men . . . by the one man's disobedience the many were made sinners.
**ROMANS 5:18-19a**

Adam's sin became our inherited sin nature. This very day, I know for sure I inherited the sin of Adam. When I was a little girl, even before I understood anything spiritual, my nature had already led me to choose sin. And hide my sin. And sin again. I imagine you also know this struggle well. We were all born with sinful natures. Like Paul in Romans 7, we know the battle inside us is real.

Let's go back to Genesis 3, because there is one more thing you must see. In verses 14-15, God pronounced a curse and a final judgment for the devil. I've tried to give some explanations here:

> Because you (the devil) have done this, cursed are you . . . I (God) will put enmity (hostility) between you (the devil) and the woman, and between your offspring and her offspring; he (Jesus, one of Eve's offspring) shall bruise your head (destroy the devil with a mortal blow), and you (the devil) shall bruise his heel (will deliver painful and vexing wounds, but they are not mortal).
> **GENESIS 3:14-15 (EXPLANATIONS ADDED)**

In Genesis 3:15, God promises to undo all that Satan has brought about. He promises a victorious Redeemer.

And don't miss this. God gave that promise to His beloved, disobedient creation *before* they were banished from the garden. My pastor has made this beautiful proclamation:

## On Adam and Eve's worst day, our God of hope promised His best day![8]

The love of God has always been greater than everything. And God's love does not change. Long before we were born, God's love already knew we could not change our nature, break the chains of our sin, or get back into His presence on our own.

So Love made a promise. Jesus Christ, our Redeemer, is Love's promise kept.

# READ AND MEDITATE

**MY DAY 3 PRAYER FOR YOU**

*O Father, You promised a Redeemer for this fallen world, and You kept Your promise in Jesus Christ. God, we bless You and thank You and rejoice in Your unfailing love. Take the truth of Your promise kept deep into our souls. You have seen our sin, and long before we knew, You promised a way to forgiveness, a way to restoration, a way to be redeemed. Move powerfully in our hearts. Open our eyes. Give new life to our prayers. Stir our souls awake. For Jesus' name, amen and amen.*

# RESPOND IN PRAYER

Oh give thanks to the LORD, for he is good,
for his steadfast love endures forever!
**PSALM 107:1**

DAY 4

# READ, MEDITATE, & PRAY

I am the one who helps you, declares the Lord; your Redeemer is the Holy One of Israel.
**ISAIAH 41:14**

## READ AND MEDITATE

*TODAY'S READING: PSALMS 7–9*

**MY DAY 4 PRAYER FOR YOU**

*Father, we feel our great need and the struggle inside. God, please be loud with Your love to every heart today. We need a Redeemer, and You have promised to redeem. Help us turn loose of every old way of coping and the broken ways we manage our pain. God, let us fall headlong into Your grace and declare with new faith that all of our hope is in You. We need You, Lord. Come quickly, sweet Redeemer. In Jesus' name, amen.*

## RESPOND IN PRAYER

He has granted to us his precious and very great promises,
so that through them you may become partakers of the divine nature.
**2 PETER 1:4**

## DAY 5

# READ, MEDITATE, & PRAY

God sent forth his Son . . . to redeem those who were under the law, so that we might receive adoption as sons.
**GALATIANS 4:4b-5**

## READ AND MEDITATE

*TODAY'S READING: PSALMS 10–12*

**MY DAY 5 PRAYER FOR YOU**

*Father, will You keep making these truths personal to us—not some far off theology, but hope for our pain right now. We cannot save ourselves, but You have declared from Your glory, "I can." Lord, speak right now, maybe in ways we've never heard. Lord, do whatever it takes to crack any hard shell of indifference. Come into our chaotic lives with Your love. Get our full attention, Lord. Make Yourself known. Be a safe place today. Send the Holy Spirit to help us ask You, "Lord, come and be my Redeemer." Oh sweet Jesus, be my Redeemer, amen.*

## RESPOND IN PRAYER

Draw near to my soul, redeem me.
**PSALM 69:18**

# SESSION 2: VIEWER GUIDE

## REDEEMED FOR A LIFE WITH GOD

> Bless the Lord, O my soul,
> and all that is within me,
> bless his holy name!
> Bless the Lord, O my soul,
> and forget not all his benefits,
> who forgives all your iniquity,
> who heals all your diseases,
> who redeems your life from the pit,
> who crowns you with steadfast love and mercy,
> who satisfies you with good
> so that your youth is renewed like the eagle's.
> **PSALM 103:1-5**

David writes this psalm in celebration of the _____ of our _____.

The first _____ of the Lord is that He forgives all of your _____.

None of the benefits of the _____ come until you've been _____ of your sin.

The consequences of Adam and Eve's sin were _____ and a _____ _____ attached to all of humanity.

> I will put enmity between you and the woman,
> and between your offspring and her offspring;
> he shall bruise your head,
> and you shall bruise his heel.
> **GENESIS 3:15**

To be redeemed means to be _____ into _____ with God.

God promises to _____ us with His _____.

Video sessions available for purchase
at *www.lifeway.com/redeemed*

# LOSING PARADISE

I realize our weeks together are going to fly by, but my heart has two big desires for us in this study:

- To know more about what we believe—*to know more about being redeemed.*
- To become better image-bearers than we've ever been—*to live everyday lives that are actually being redeemed.*

Someone once told me that acquiring knowledge is like learning to read a map. On any given subject, the first things to learn are the big things. With a map of the United States, you'd begin with the big features, like the names of oceans, mountains, states and their capitals. Next, you could learn the major interstates, then focus on one area at a time, learning the state roads, county names, and neighborhoods. If you found a really interesting place, you could dig and dig until you knew every little pig path.

To put your mind at ease, this *Redeemed* study is mostly going to stay with the big interstate ideas. Every once in a while, we may stop for a scenic overlook—especially if I think we've come to a place where you might want to look around—but I'd be sick if you close this book and only have a better Bible map of redemption. God's Word is so much more than a road map! The truth of His Word has the power to radically transform every part of our lives. Because God wants to redeem our lives, you and I really can live every day better than before. With that in mind, let's begin today with prayer,

> *Father, teach me Your truth today. Inspire me. Renew me. Rearrange me. I want to listen for Your voice as I'm learning. Help me to pay attention while I study and not be stubborn when the Holy Spirit nudges my heart or shows me something new. Give me a new strength—one I've never had—to want to obey You quickly. I want to know Your truth and become better because of it. In the precious name of Jesus, amen.*

Last week, we ended our study at the entrance to the garden of Eden where a cherubim stood guard at the gate. Adam and Eve had disobeyed God. God made a promise to redeem. Then, Adam and Eve were banished from the garden. With paradise at their backs, they walked toward their sad new reality: the consequences of their sin. They went:

From blessings to curses.
From life to death.

From living in the perfect presence of God to separation and living in the presence of evil.

As our representative, Adam sinned, and nothing would ever be the same for all humanity. We began our study with Adam and Eve because the story of redemption began unfolding when God made a promise to restore the broken relationship.

We could just keep chugging along down this road, moving toward the way God kept His promise, but I think it may be helpful to pull off the interstate and go back into the garden for just a bit. Maybe you have some bigger questions that we flew right past. Like, *What just happened in there? And why in the world did God allow it?* God created you with an amazing mind, so let's begin giving ourselves and others, permission to wrestle with truth until it settles in your heart. Do you have questions about the garden of Eden? The first sin? Satan?

*Write any questions you have here.*

Let's take a couple of days and tackle some questions about the garden of Eden. Things like, *Why did God create humankind in the first place? If we were created perfect, why did Adam choose sin?* And tomorrow, *Where did Satan come from? Why was Satan in the garden if it was perfect?*

*Here we go. Open your Bible and turn to Isaiah 43:6-7 (ESV). Fill in the blanks below.*

*Bring my _____ from afar and my _____ from the end of the earth, everyone who is called by my name, whom I created _____ _____ _____, whom I formed and made.*

**All your questions are allowed when you're studying the Bible! Too many people have questions or doubts but don't seek God for the answers, so they just sit and stew in the muck of not knowing or understanding. It's exciting when someone full of questions begins to search for truth. I love watching God answer the honest seeker! If you have questions about God or the Bible, then ask Him to help you. He says to all of us, *Bring Me your questions!***

*"You will seek me and find me, when you seek me with all your heart"* (Jer. 29:13).

*Now, turn to Psalm 19:1-2 (ESV) and fill in the blanks below:*

*The heavens declare _____ _____ _____ _____, and the sky above proclaims his handiwork. Day to day pours out speech, and night to night reveals knowledge.*

*According to these verses, how would you answer these questions:*

*Why did God create the earth and humanity?*

*Why did God create you?*

**Along with the gift of Jesus as our Savior, free will is a gift central to Christianity. Free will makes Christianity a relationship, instead of just another religion with a list of do's and don'ts. No one is coerced to follow Christ. You freely accept the invitation to be a Christian. You freely choose to obey Christ's teachings or not. This wonderful gift should never be taken for granted.**

Adam and Eve were created with a perfect nature, placed in a perfect environment, and assigned to rule over the perfect creation. God assigned Adam to be the master over creation, but Adam was still accountable to God. God gave Adam this instruction to obey.

And the Lord God commanded the man, "You are free to eat from any tree in the garden; but you must not eat from the tree of the knowledge of good and evil, for when you eat from it you will certainly die."
**GENESIS 2:16-17 (NIV)**

*Underline the first three words of God's command to Adam.*

God gave the perfect man the perfect freedom to choose. Having the freedom to choose is a good gift that continues for all humans to this day. We call this gift our "free will."

No one *made* Adam and Eve sin. No one forced their decision. Even though Satan came into the garden, and even though they were tempted, the responsibility was clear: Adam and Eve freely chose to disobey God. Human freedom means having the ability to cause your own actions. If someone or something forces you to choose, then you are not free. God made man free to choose, even free to choose the possibility of evil. Adam was created with the power to obey or disobey.

Free will is the same for us today. We are created with the ability to make meaningful, moral choices. God has instructed us, but He does not force us to love Him, obey Him, or follow Him. All people are free but will also be accountable to our Creator.

God instructed Adam not to choose wrongly, when He said:

> **But you must not** eat from the tree of the
> knowledge of good and evil . . .
> **GENESIS 2:17a (NIV, EMPHASIS MINE)**

We all know how Adam used his free will. His sin was an act of disobedience, unbelief, and disloyalty—and in Genesis 3, God held Adam responsible:

> Have you eaten of the tree of which I commanded you not to eat?
> **GENESIS 3:11b**

At the very moment of Adam and Eve's disobedience, sin came to earth, and a transition began in creation called "the fall." Adam and Eve fell from innocence. They fell from favor with God. They fell from perfection and from life to death. The fall in the garden of Eden set the course for the rest of humanity.

When I think about the choice Adam and Eve made in the garden, I want to be mad at both of them. But the very second I think, *I'd never choose disobedience over God*, my conscience screams back at me, *Liar*. Many times I have chosen disobedience over God's instruction. Truth is, all sin is ultimately irrational. It didn't make sense for Adam and Eve to trust the deception of Satan and doubt God. And rebellion against God's instruction still doesn't make sense today.

Today, you and I must remember that we still have a very real Enemy who would love to see us fail. That failure probably won't begin with a huge choice, but something more like a compromise. A hedge on the truth. Then a cover-up. And on toward deceit.

> *Is there anything in your life, currently, that feels like "just an apple," but is in fact, the beginning of a compromise?*

Man's *disobedience* was the fruit of unbelief. His *obedience* would have been the fruit of faith.

Eve was deceived into thinking she needed to know why God had forbidden the fruit of the tree. If she had trusted God, His Words of instruction to her would have been sufficient.

God wants our obedience by faith. Responding in obedience to God is not based on always understanding why God says what He says or does what He does. We are called to obedience based on *who* God is.

*When God graciously reveals to us an area of compromise, how should we respond?*

*Sometimes people do not respond quickly to a revealed area of disobedience or compromise. Why do you think that happens? Explain.*

*Take a minute to consider your own relationship with God. Place an "X" along the line to mark where you are today.*

|————————————————————————————————|

*Not following God*                              *Devoted follower of God*

|————————————————————————————————|

*Can't trust God*                              *Trusting God is all I have*

|————————————————————————————————|

*Disobedient to God*                              *Quick to obey God*

Sometimes, instead of quick obedience, we can lean into unbelief, deciding that we will not obey God until we know *why*.

*Are there places in your life where God has been asking you to obey Him by faith? Explain.*

What if today is the day you begin trusting *who* God is and *what* He has said instead of demanding answers to all your whys? As you know from today's study, God has created you with the freedom to choose as you please, but what if there is more to this faith thing than you've understood? What if trusting God, even when you don't have all the answers to every why, is the way He is most glorified? The way He wants to redeem your heart? The way He wants to bless your life?

*Is there one very real step you can freely choose to turn toward God today?*

# READ AND MEDITATE

*TODAY'S READING: PSALMS 13–15*

### MY DAY 6 PRAYER FOR YOU

*God, I pray for my sweet friend, that chains of disobedience will be broken today. She has been created to declare Your glory with her life. I hope she can see that knowing You more is the way to trusting You more. That obedience by faith is the path of blessing. Peace. Grace. Rest. Father, will You give her a greater confidence about the truth of the Bible? Send the Holy Spirit to show her how to trust You more. Will You help her rearrange her life around the truth of who You are, and then, Lord, will You bless every act of her obedience? In Jesus' name, amen.*

# RESPOND IN PRAYER

When Jesus described the intimacy He wants with us, He talked about joining us for dinner.

> Behold, I stand at the door and knock. If anyone hears my voice and opens the door, I will come in to him and eat with him, and he with me.
> **REVELATION 3:20**

A praying life feels like our family mealtimes because prayer is all about relationship. It's intimate and hints at eternity. We don't think about communication or words but about whom we are talking with. . . . Many people struggle to learn how to pray because they are focusing on praying, not on God. Making prayer the center is like making conversation the center of a family mealtime. . . . [It's] like trying to drive while looking at the windshield instead of through it. It freezes us, making us unsure of where to go.[1]
**PAUL MILLER**

---
---
---
---
---
---
---
---
---
---
---
---
---
---
---
---

DAY 7

# THE FIRST SINNER

Let's begin today with a word of caution from C.S. Lewis:

**There are two equal and opposite errors into which our race can fall about the devils. One is to disbelieve in their existence. The other is to believe, and to feel an excessive and unhealthy interest in them. They themselves are equally pleased by both errors, and hail a materialist or magician with the same delight.**[2]

You'll remember that yesterday, we pulled over in the garden of Eden to address a few questions. Today we're looking at, *Where did Satan come from? Why was Satan in the garden if it was perfect?*

We're packing a good bit into today's study, so let's pray before we dive in.

*Father, thank You for the revelation You give us in Your Word. Thank You for Jesus, who died to pay for my sin and defeat Satan for all eternity. Teach me today. I want more understanding. More peace. More of You. In the powerful name of Jesus, amen.*

It's completely understandable to have questions about Satan and his demons. To address them, we are going to stay with what God has said and the saints have seen, as recorded in the Scriptures. Sometimes, we are afraid to consider the reality of Satan until we are equipped with the truth of God's power.

Satan, as you may know, was an angel, created by God. Theologian Wayne Grudem defined angels as "created spiritual beings with moral judgment and high intelligence but without physical bodies."[3]

*Read Psalm 148:2-5. When God commanded, what was created?*

*Turn to Genesis 1:31a, and fill in the blanks below.*

*And God saw everything that he had made, and behold, it was _____ _____.*

All that God created in the universe was perfect and good, but angels are spiritual beings, created with the same free will as humans. At the creation of the angelic world, there was no evil nor demons, but by the time God created Adam and Eve in the garden, there had been a rebellion in heaven. According to Ezekiel, Satan was an anointed guardian cherub who covers or guards.

> You were an anointed guardian cherub. I placed you; you were on the
> holy mountain of God; in the midst of the stones of fire you walked.
> **EZEKIEL 28:14**

But Satan was corrupted by his own beauty.

> Your heart was proud because of your beauty; you corrupted
> your wisdom for the sake of your splendor.
> **EZEKIEL 28:17a**

Isaiah 14:12-15 is a possible reference to the fall of Satan from heaven. His traditional name, Lucifer, is taken from the passage below.

> How you are fallen from heaven, O Day Star [Lucifer], Son of Dawn! . . . You
> said in your heart, "I will ascend to heaven; above the stars of God I will set
> my throne on high; I will sit on the mount of assembly in the far reaches of the
> north; I will ascend above the heights of the clouds; I will make myself like the
> Most High." But you are brought down to Sheol, to the far reaches of the pit.
> **ISAIAH 14:12-15**

Most Bible scholars believe these verses in Isaiah refer to the king of Babylon, but the New Testament (Luke 10:18; 1 Tim. 3:6) seems to infer this king made the same choices as the first archangel, committing the sin of pride and trying to be equal to God. Sometimes you'll hear someone say, "Pride was the original sin," and this is what they're referring to. It was the pride of Satan that made him the first sinner. He wanted to be like God. Actually, he wanted to be more than God; He wanted to replace God.

Some people consider pride a "low-level" sin, or a private sin that doesn't really hurt anyone but the offender. As with Satan, pride may begin privately in the heart, but left unchecked, it becomes the sin that wrecks lives, relationships, even nations. Pride begins inside us with selfish motives. An exaggerated ego. A low opinion of others. A distorted view of reality. Disrespect for God.

**The vice I am talking of is Pride or Self-Conceit: and the virtue opposite to it, in Christian morals, is called Humility . . . According to Christian teachers, the essential vice, the utmost evil, is Pride. Unchastity, anger, greed, drunkenness, and all that, are mere flea bites in comparison: it was through Pride that the devil became the devil: Pride leads to every other vice: it is the complete anti-God state of mind.[4]**
**C.S. LEWIS**

The Book of Proverbs says:

Pride goes before destruction, and a haughty spirit before a fall.
**PROVERBS 16:18**

*When you consider the sin of pride in your own life, do you see places where your pride became a wrecking ball of pain and destruction? Explain.*

*Before we go on, ask God to reveal any pride hidden in your heart. Ask for His forgiveness and help to rid your life of the chains of pride.*

I'm sorry to tell you, but the bad news about Satan continues. Revelation 12:3-9 says a third of the created angels followed Satan in his prideful rebellion. Those angels who followed Satan are called demons. Satan and his demons were once good angels who sinned and lost their place with God (see 2 Pet. 2:4; Jude 6). Now as fallen, evil angels, demons continue to work evil in the world.

Let's review:

- The leader of the angelic rebellion was Satan. You can call him the first sinner. We first meet Satan in the garden (Gen. 3) as the serpent who tempts Eve to sin.

- There was sin in the universe before there was sin on earth. Remember, the first sinner was in heaven when he rebelled.

- There is sin on earth because Adam chose the evil of disobedience with his own free will.

Quick heart check: How are you doing with all this Satan stuff? This is one time I hope Bible knowledge is giving you a real and immediate peace. Satan and all his demons are not bigger than God. God is their Creator, and the rest of their story is going to unfold! Choose your response to the following:

|  | Yes | No | Still thinking about it |
|---|---|---|---|
| Evil is real. |  |  |  |
| Angels are real. |  |  |  |
| Satan is real. |  |  |  |
| Angels and demons are present on earth. |  |  |  |

Okay, deep breath. This theology is about to get hard. Not hard like big words that are difficult to understand. I mean hard like the Bible is silent. For me, that's the hardest kind of hard. Here we go.

### GOD DID NOT CREATE EVIL.

His work is perfect, for all his ways are justice. A God of faithfulness and without iniquity, just and right is he.
DEUTERONOMY 32:4

God made man upright, but they have sought out many schemes.
ECCLESIASTES 7:29

### NOR DID GOD CREATE SATAN WITH AN EVIL NATURE.

Far be it from God that he should do wickedness, and from the Almighty that he should do wrong.
JOB 34:10

God cannot be tempted with evil, and he himself tempts no one.
JAMES 1:13b

**GOD DOES NOT PRODUCE EVIL.**

> Your heavenly Father is perfect.
> **MATTHEW 5:48b**

> You who are of purer eyes than to see evil and cannot look at wrong.
> **HABAKKUK 1:13**

However, God does permit sin and evil to occur.

Surely your heart just asked, *Why? Why would a good God, who can foresee all things, allow evil to exist? With the power to prevent the fall of humanity, why would God allow it?*

Evil began with the irrational choice of an angel. *Angelic insanity.* A multitude of other angels followed. *Angelic insanity, multiplied.* The first man made the same irrational choice to sin. The sin nature was transmitted to the entire human race.

Evil in this world is not an accident, nor was it unforeseen by God. Why God allows sin has been debated since Adam and Eve heard the garden gate lock shut behind them. Yet, why God's sovereign purpose allows evil remains a mystery without sufficient answers.

Sin was, and still is, an irrational and unreasonable choice. Maybe it's impossible to explain unreasonable actions with legitimate reasoning. Either way, the contradiction will not be settled today. Answers about why are not yet ours. Here's what we know:

> Let both [weeds and wheat] grow together until the harvest, and at harvest time I will tell the reapers, Gather the weeds first and bind them in bundles to be burned, but gather the wheat into my barn.
> **MATTHEW 13:30**

> He has fixed a day on which he will judge the world in righteousness by a man whom he has appointed; and of this he has given assurance to all by raising him from the dead.
> **ACTS 17:31**

Evil must continue along with good until it reaches God's determined end. Then, the evil will be judged and banished forever.

Sometimes the *why* questions of God do not find their complete answers. Remember yesterday and the unbelief that came to Eve because she wanted to know why when God had asked her to trust?

*Does it bother you not to have a neat-and-tidy answer for evil? Why or why not?*

*Can you still trust God if you don't completely understand all His ways? Why or why not?*

Evil is real. The devil and his demons continue to be active here on earth. But, he does not win. As with everything in the Bible, we have to read the rest of the story. God has a future plan for Satan, too.

> . . . and the devil who had deceived them was thrown into the lake of fire and sulfur where the beast and the false prophet were, and they will be tormented day and night forever and ever.
> **REVELATION 20:10**

*Turn to Romans 16:20 and write Paul's words here:*

_____

_____

_____

_____

_____

_____

> The thief comes only to steal and kill and destroy. I came that they may have life and have it abundantly.
> **JOHN 10:10**

No reference to the Devil or devils is included in any Christian Creeds, and it is quite possible to be a Christian without believing in them. I do believe such beings exist, but that is my own affair. Supposing there to be such beings, the degree to which humans were conscious of their presence would presumably vary very much. I mean, the more a man was in the Devil's power, the less he would be aware of it, on the principle that a man is still fairly sober as long as he knows he's drunk. It is the people who are fully awake and trying hard to be good who would be most aware of the Devil.[5]
C.S. LEWIS

# READ AND MEDITATE

**MY DAY 7 PRAYER FOR YOU**

*Father, I pray today is a day of certainty—certainty concerning the presence of evil, and yet a greater certainty in Your awesome power. Lord, give us the security to live in a world full of evil without falling into fear and despair. Protect our very lives. Hide us underneath Your wings. Guard our comings and our goings. Wrap the shield of Your steadfast love around us. We long for the abundant life You have promised us in Jesus, amen and amen.*

# RESPOND IN PRAYER

Our prayers thus lay the track down on which God's power can come. Like some mighty locomotive, His power is irresistible, but it cannot reach us without rails.[6]
**WATCHMAN NEE**

DAY 8

# SEPARATION, SIN, AND DEATH

After yesterday's study, I'm really grateful you decided to come back! Truth is, the past two days have been downright depressing. Here are a few reasons why:

> We had paradise, but lost it.
> We had innocence before God. Gone.
> We had an intimate friendship with God. Lost that, too.
> We inherited a sin nature through no choice of our own (but we would've chosen it too).
> We now live with the consequence of sin called death.
> And if all that's not bad enough—we found out God has sovereignly allowed Satan and his demons to live and work here on earth.

So, there you go. The back story on redemption is pretty awful. But before you shoot the messenger for reporting the facts, let me tell you the good news: we can't really get any lower than we are.

Feel better?

I'm smiling right now because I know you want me to move us along and get onto something else. Trust me, I can only smile about us being uncomfortable because I know where we're headed. This whole thing's gonna take a turn real soon, I promise. Actually, my promise has nothing to do with it. This study is getting ready to take a turn because God made a promise—and then He kept it.

We've done some pretty decent Bible study during the past couple of days. If someone asked you how sin entered the world, you should be able to tell him or her what the Bible says. If they asked you about the fall, or the consequences of sin, you should be able to tell them what happened. Too many people are out there misrepresenting God, mainly because they've never been taught what the Bible says. As followers of Jesus, we need to know the truth and learn to represent it correctly and plainly.

But we're not rushing along today because I want us to examine the truth we have learned in light of our own everyday lives.

There is a weird, unsettled awareness I've known from time to time. Surely, you've felt it too. Sometimes when I'm quiet, still, or sad, my soul reminds me that things aren't the way

John Calvin called what happened to human nature, *total depravity* or *total inability,* meaning the effects of the fall extend to every part of our personalities—our thinking, emotions, and will. Sin has extended to our entire being.

The heart is deceitful above all things, and desperately sick; who can understand it?
JEREMIAH 17:9

Therefore, just as sin came into the world through one man, and death through sin, and so death spread to all men because all sinned.
ROMANS 5:12

The consequences of Adam's transgression for the human race are the imputation of his sin to all his descendants, their consequent liability to death, and their inheritance of a depraved nature.[7]

they should be. Something is missing or not how it is supposed to be. Even on my very best days, that vague, hollow feeling can still appear. Sometimes, it has been a deep, dark place, and at other times, a momentary, passing haze. Something like a reminder for the soul.

*In what times or situations are you acutely aware of your own "hollow soul"?*

The emptiness in our souls was produced by the fall. Yep, that same stinkin' fall from the garden of Eden. Remember:

Humanity was created:
- in the image of God,
- to enjoy a relationship with God, and
- to reign and rule over the earth.

At the fall:
- sin entered human nature,
- sin separated humankind from the presence God on earth, and
- sin eternally separated humanity from God in death.

But your iniquities have made a separation between you and your God.
ISAIAH 59:2a

No one has ever said to me, "Hey, can we talk? I'm really struggling with those consequences from the fall. I'm harboring some anger toward Adam and Eve for choosing to sin. I'm feeling depressed because they set me up and lost my paradise. My life would have been great, but Adam had to go and sin."

Do you know why no one talks like that? Because it's not really about Adam and Eve anymore. Their sin got them kicked out of the garden, but right here in my house, this afternoon, it's about me. I was born with a soul separated from God. I can feel its emptiness. Some days the ache comes like waves. No one has to keep talking to me about Adam's sin because he may have blown it. Here's the bigger deal in my little world: I've blown it, too, and I still do. I have a sin nature. And I hate it.

> If we say we have not sinned, we make him
> a liar, and his word is not in us.
> **1 JOHN 1:10**

Truth is, nobody really talks like this anymore. *Separated from God. Sin nature. Depravity. Guaranteed death.* Some say those old Bible words might offend. Honestly, most people would rather not think about it.

But everywhere you look, you can see that humanity is still separated from God, and our sin nature hasn't gone anywhere. Even if people don't want to talk about it, something is off, and we know it. We know we are lonely. We know we are guilty. We know we're going to die. And we know everybody is desperately trying to find something to fill the hole in their hearts.

*Separation, sin, and death are a lot more than Bible words; they are my reality. They are your reality. Are any of these struggles familiar to you? Check any that you've faced.*

- ☐ *The fear of missing out on something or someone better.*
- ☐ *The inability to make commitments and keep them.*
- ☐ *Lacking enough self-discipline to do better.*
- ☐ *Lacking the inner strength to rebound after being left-out, uninvited, fired, or ignored.*
- ☐ *Feeling a stifled, ever-present anxiety that your life is missing real purpose or meaning.*
- ☐ *Missing an internal anchor that grounds the soul, no matter what comes.*
- ☐ *Playing the victim card often—maybe because it's true and maybe because it's all you've got.*
- ☐ *Being quick to take offense over anything, becoming irritated, fed up, or peeved.*
- ☐ *Playing new versions of the comparison game, yet each one just keeps stealing more joy.*

**What can we learn about sin from Adam and Eve in the garden?**

1. **Sin is defined by God and not naturally grasped by the mind of humankind. We must trust God's definition of sin.**

2. **Our senses cannot be trusted to discern sin. Many times, evil looks desirable.**

3. **A seemingly insignificant sin can have wide-spread repercussions.**

4. **Sin resists God's purposes, but never succeeds in overcoming them.**

5. **Sin seeks to oppose God.**[8]

These may be the days of a new culture with new technology and new achievements, but the symptoms of the fall remain. We were made to enjoy God and reign with Him, but here in the new culture, we still suffer the effects of separation, sin, and death.

The Bible explains how we got here, and I can testify to the reality of my own sin. I have felt the ache in my soul telling me something is missing.

We are the hippest, coolest, most intellectual, most relevant, most connected people this earth has ever known. Yet one glaring thing has not changed since the garden of Eden. We are born into a sin nature and act like sinners until we are forgiven and redeemed by the blood of Jesus.

No one has ever been able to escape the grip of sin apart from the power of Jesus Christ.

> None is righteous, no, not one; no one understands; no one seeks for God. All have turned aside; together they have become worthless; no one does good, not even one.
> ROMANS 3:10-12

*How are you able to see that what the Bible says about separation, sin, and death is true in your own life?*

*How do you see it in your life experiences so far? In the feelings in your soul?*

*What about this very day and the challenges you face?*

When I come face to face with my own sin, and the sin of this world, I am sure that what the Bible says about us is true. Our sin separates us from God. And if that were the end of the story, I am sure I wouldn't be able to survive.

But, oh, hallelujah, God has not left us in this helpless place. I can't wait to meet you in these pages tomorrow!

# READ AND MEDITATE

*TODAY'S READING: PSALMS 19–21*

**MY DAY 8 PRAYER FOR YOU**

*Father, will You do that grace-filled, Holy Spirit thing that You do? Will You convict us of our sin as You also extend the hope of being redeemed? God, will You prompt and prod and do whatever it takes to encourage my friend to seek You personally? For her soul. Her forgiveness. Her needs. Her future. Will You keep her studying Your Bible everyday, even when the news is real and the truth is brutally discouraging? God, will You reach down into the most sinful places of the heart and do the work only You can do? Redeemer. Healer. Savior. Lord, amen.*

# RESPOND IN PRAYER

The more we pray, the more we shall want to pray. The more we pray, the more we can pray. The more we pray, the more we shall pray. He who prays little will pray less, but he who prays much will pray more.[9]
**C.H. SPURGEON**

## DAY 9

# UNSHAKABLY COMMITTED

**Welcome to the turn in the road. Hallelujah, we're finally here!**

Today is the day everything in this study is about to change. You're probably ready to get on with more of the redeemed life like I am. The past few days of sin and separation have been heavy stuff. But I promise you this, if you will take hold of these truths, both for yourself and for the people you meet, the next time someone asks, *Why do I need to be redeemed? Who can be redeemed? Why is sin such a big deal? Where did sin come from anyway?* Girl, you are going to know what to tell them!

Almost every day, I ask the Lord to teach me how to teach the gospel more clearly. Patiently. Biblically. Gracefully. Learning what it means to be redeemed is the same as learning how to explain the gospel. And you are learning the gospel!

Let's recap the basics so far:

> The law of the LORD is perfect, reviving the soul; the testimony of the LORD is sure, making wise the simple; the precepts of the LORD are right, rejoicing the heart; the commandment of the LORD is pure, enlightening the eyes.
> **PSALM 19:7-8**

- We were created for perfect relationship with God.
- Adam and Eve disobeyed God and broke their relationship with Him.
- Their sin became our sin nature.
- Their consequences became our inheritance.
- Today, every person is born with a sin nature and its consequences, appointed to live out their days in a fallen body on a fallen earth.

What if, after everything we've just learned, the Bible said,

The God who created man in His image saw what they had done with His steadfast love. So He hardened His heart and stomped out of their universe, off toward eternity without them. As He turned to leave them helpless and alone, the angels heard Him mutter to the heavenly beings, "I gave them life and all of my love. I only required one act of obedience. They deserve their consequences and more."

What if here is where the Bible read: THE END.

I felt sick just making up those words. Even more sad is knowing that lots of people live every day with a very real kind of sickness called hopelessness. These are not just the people who live somewhere far away. There are people living in your apartment building and working in cubicles next to yours who may not study the Bible or know how to speak the name of God, but their souls tell them something is wrong. From somewhere inside, they know everything is broken. Every, single thing. And beyond the brokenness, people can decide they're being punished in some weird cosmic way, and if there ever was a God, He has long since turned away.

No wonder people who don't know God live the way they do. Choose the way they choose. Act the way they act. When people don't know the rest of the story, all they can see is brokenness. Life is without hope. No one can be trusted. All you have is yourself.

*I meet a lot of people who live without God who are quick to be offended and bound up in anger. As you think about the people in your own life, what characteristics do you see in the lives of those who live without God?*

I'm not always on my game, but trying to remember how people act and respond apart from God is one of the ways God is giving me a heart of mercy for difficult people. Goodness, I'm not sure how I would act if I only believed I'd been left here to suffer punishment.

That's exactly why the love of God is such good news. The whole wide world needs to know that God did not take His love and stomp off into oblivion. That's exactly why we're in a hurry to make this turn in the study. You and I both know redemption is coming, and when you know what's coming, you want to hurry up and get there!

The Bible describes the kind of relationship God wants with His people as a covenant relationship. A covenant always involves two things:

1. A relationship between two parties
2. A commitment from both parties to certain responsibilities.

Today, we use the word in several ways: marriage covenant, legal covenant, real estate covenant, covenant nations, and so forth. The definition below does a great job of pulling together the biblical theology concerning covenant.

*Covenant* refers to the act of God in freely establishing a mutually binding relationship with humankind. Through the covenant God bestows blessings on humans in conditional and unconditional terms. Conditionally, God blesses humans as they obey the terms of the covenant. Unconditionally, God bestows blessings on humans regardless of their obedience or disobedience to the terms of the covenant. God made covenants with Noah, Abraham, Moses, and David. But above all, God has fulfilled these covenants.[10]

*Answer the following questions using the definition above.*

*Who initiated the covenant relationship between God and humanity?*

*What are the two kinds of blessings God gives to humanity through the covenant?*

*What are some of the blessings of God you have experienced through your own obedience to God?*

*What are some of the undeserved blessings God has granted to you through His unconditional covenant love?*

The Bible implies (Hosea 6:7) that God initiated a covenant with humanity at creation. The sin of Adam and Eve broke the covenant. And as you know, with two human beings or two human nations, a broken covenant would normally be *the end* of the relationship.

The end of a marriage
The end of a business
The end of a peace agreement.

But, God's ways are higher than our ways, and here is where our study turns.

Adam and Eve broke covenant with God.
Sin entered. Consequences entered. Eternal separation entered.
Each one of us has sinned, and each one of us has broken covenant with God.
*But, God has not broken covenant with us.*

I just put down my computer, stood up here in my little writing room, and danced around the floor. Did you just get that? God did *not* break covenant with us. And He *has not* broken covenant with us. The sin of humanity did not discourage God or turn Him away.

> I will put enmity between you and the woman, and between your offspring and her offspring; he shall bruise your head, and you shall bruise his heel.
> **GENESIS 3:15**

Do you remember Genesis 3:15, when God promised to send a Redeemer who would destroy evil and restore His covenant relationship with His people? And then there was one of the worst days ever in Genesis 3:24-25—the cherubim with a flaming-sword blocking the entrance to the garden and Adam and Eve with their backs to paradise.

Take a minute to turn to a passage in between: Genesis 3:21. Just before God enforces the consequences of their disobedience, God does this:

> Therefore the Lord God sent him out from the garden of Eden to work the ground from which he was taken. He drove out the man, and at the east of the garden of Eden he placed the cherubim and a flaming sword that turned every way to guard the way to the tree of life.
> **GENESIS 3:23-24**

> *And the Lord God _____ for Adam and for his wife _____ of _____ and _____ them.*

Adam and Eve's sin revealed to them their nakedness. But in the face of sin, evil, and shame, God made fine leather clothing for His beloved. Even in His discipline, God chose to cover Adam and Eve with His love.

## The Covenants of God

If you dig a little deeper into this covenant time line, you'll see God's faithfulness to keep His covenants, even when humanity was unfaithful.

1. Creation Covenant (Gen. 1–2): God's original plan revealed

Sin enters the world, and yet God promises a Redeemer.

2. Noahic Covenant (Gen. 9): for life after the flood

3. Abrahamic Covenant (Gen. 12–17): for life after Babel

4. Mosaic/Sinai/Israeli Covenant (Ex. 19–24)

5. Davidic Covenant (2 Sam. 7)

6. New Covenant (Jer. 31): a new covenant is promised

The New Covenant is fulfilled in the Person of Jesus Christ and belongs to all people who trust in Him (Heb. 9:15,27-28).

Why? Why would God extend such a love to Adam and Eve? And why would He continue to keep loving faithless people all through the Old Testament? I love this answer from Palmer Robertson:

**The answer is found in the concept of "covenant." God is *unshakably committed* to His creation, to His human creatures, and to His plans for both. God did not make junk, and He will not junk what He made! He is lovingly-loyal and loyally-loving to the works of His hands. He loves what He is committed to; He is committed to what He loves! So, when it all fell into trouble, God's desire was not to annihilate and destroy it, but to save and restore it.**

**God, in other words, has a covenant with creation from which He will never turn back! His dedication to His world is irrevocable.**[11]

Why would God choose to redeem? Because His covenant love is unshakably committed to His creation.

To this very day—no matter where you are, what you have done or should have done, what you are hiding or how blatantly you have committed sin in the face of God—God's love for you is not broken.

The study just took a turn in the road because God's covenant love to you is not broken. The Promise Maker is also the Promise Keeper. The love that created you is the love that continues to pursue you. The Bible calls it the steadfast love of God.

Most people who hear about God don't make the turn toward His love, and I'll tell you why. We can all nod our heads and agree to the reality of our own sin nature. We may not understand it, but we sense our separation from God. Most of us even know we've caused it, and we can all do a pretty good job of beating ourselves up with the guilt and shame of it all.

It's so hard to turn and receive the undeserved, unearned, steadfast love of God. The same Satan who was in the garden is screaming, "You don't deserve it," and he's right. But not deserving God's love is the whole stinkin' point of being redeemed. Deserving God's love is not a prerequisite for receiving His love. Never has been. Never will be.

The God who created you has not wavered. HE LOVES YOU—still.

# READ AND MEDITATE

*TODAY'S READING: PSALMS 22–24*

**MY DAY 9 PRAYER FOR YOU**

*Oh Father, tell her You are not far off. Tell her You keep Your covenant. Tell her she's worth crossing heaven and earth for. Tell her nothing will ever shake Your commitment. Tell her the redeemed can never again be separated from Your love. Tell her over and over until she believes. Tell her again, Lord, tell her again. Amen and amen and amen.*

# RESPOND IN PRAYER

Don't hunt for a feeling in prayer. Deep in our psyches we want an experience with God or an experience in prayer. Once we make that our quest, we lose God. You don't experience God; you get to know Him. You submit to Him. You enjoy Him. He is, after all, a person.[12]
**PAUL E. MILLER**

DAY 10

# THE PLAN

Hello, friend.

Are you still trying to take yesterday's truth down into your soul?

> The steadfast love of the LORD never ceases; his mercies never come to an end;
> they are new every morning; great is your faithfulness.
> **LAMENTATIONS 3:22-23**

Honestly, I hope we never get over it. I hope we never stop being amazed or humbled by the steadfast love of God. Do you believe God loves you with a steadfast, covenant love?

I'm not trying to be hokey with what I am about to ask you to do. I have such a distaste for "cheesy," especially with regard to teaching the Bible. But sometimes, something is important enough to ask you to stretch a little. Saying something out loud can be like underlining a truth for your soul. Will you say this aloud to God:

> *God, I believe that You love me with a steadfast love. I want to receive Your love for me with gratefulness and humility.*

If you can't yet say that, will you say:

> *God, will You help me believe Your steadfast love is meant even for me? And then, will You, God, help me to receive Your love?*

To believe we are included in God's steadfast love requires a humility and a surrender. I meet women who can believe a truth for someone else but just won't believe it for themselves. Do you know how I know they don't believe for themselves? Their lives and their choices do not reflect God's love.

- A woman who believes she has been forgiven begins to live like she is forgiven. She responds to others like a forgiven woman.

- A woman who believes she is loved begins to live in the strength and security of being loved. She wants to return and multiply God's love.

- A woman who believes she has a home in heaven begins to live like she's going home.

*Receiving God's love means learning to lay down our defenses. Our doubts. Our rebellion. Do you need to surrender anything to believe God's love is meant for you?*

*What reasons do you hear other people give when they refuse to believe or accept the love of God?*

Love is God's motive; relationship is His goal; glory is His purpose. And so, long before the fall, God had a plan:

A plan to redeem His beloved from the consequences of sin,
A plan to restore our relationship with Him, and
A plan to be glorified every time someone freely chooses His love.

Let's start with a few thoughts about God's plan to redeem.

### EVEN BEFORE GOD CREATED THE WORLD, HE MADE A PLAN TO REDEEM THE WORLD.

This Jesus, delivered up according to the definite plan and foreknowledge of God, you crucified and killed by the hands of lawless men. God raised him up, loosing the pangs of death, because it was not possible for him to be held by it.
**ACTS 2:23-24**

Blessed be the God and Father of our Lord Jesus Christ, who has blessed us in Christ with every spiritual blessing in the heavenly places, even as he chose us in him before the foundation of the world, that we should be holy and blameless before him.
**EPHESIANS 1:3-4**

*According to the Ephesians passage above, when did God make His rescue plan? Why is that important?*

**IN THAT PLAN, GOD BOTH ANTICIPATED AND ALLOWED THE CHOICES THAT WOULD LEAD TO SIN AND SUFFERING, EVEN THE SUFFERING OF HIS ONLY SON, JESUS.**

For a lot of us, me included, this is one of the hardest Bible truths to accept. God foreknew the choice Adam and Eve would make, yet in His sovereignty, He allowed it to happen. God allowed the sin that brought monumental consequences, curses, and suffering.

*How do you respond to knowing that a loving God allows suffering?*

☐ *This is the reason I don't speak to God.*
☐ *This hurts me and makes me doubt.*
☐ *I am learning to trust Him, even about suffering.*
☐ *I have suffered much and, through it, know God more.*
☐ *I know He loves me. I trust Him with my suffering. He's my grace and my hope.*

Beloved, do not be surprised at the fiery trial when it comes upon you to test you, as though something strange were happening to you. But rejoice insofar as you share Christ's sufferings, that you may also rejoice and be glad when his glory is revealed.
**1 PETER 4:12-13**

In His hands, suffering can be one of the ways God delivers blessings to our lives.

Suffering can become the backdrop for His grace.
Suffering can lead us to repentance.
Suffering can reconcile us to God and renew our faith.
Suffering can draw us into deeper relationship with God.
Suffering can teach us about grace, hope, and eternity.

*Have you known blessings from God through your own suffering? Explain.*

Why did God allow the fall with its consequences and suffering? The Bible doesn't give us an answer. In the mystery of why, the Bible only tells us what we need to know: God is in control. We have a certain hope. One day, the consequences will be undone.

**GOD'S PLAN TO REDEEM WASN'T A PLAN TO TAKE US BACK TO THE PARADISE WE LOST AT THE FALL.**

With God's plan,
Jesus becomes a better Adam.
The way of grace and forgiveness becomes the better way.
Forgiven sinners become a new creation.

The new heaven and new earth are our promised better paradise.
The path of redemption brings God greater glory.

## THE PROMISED PLAN IS FULFILLED THROUGH THE WILLING SURRENDER AND SACRIFICE OF GOD'S SON, JESUS.

*Turn to Philippians 2. Read verses 6-8 and write the verbs used to describe what Jesus did for us below.*

Let's pull over here for a second and do some honest talking. Truth is, if we were running the universe, we'd probably do some things differently. For starters, evil, war, and hate—they'd all be outta here.

This is where I need to officially disqualify myself from Universe Creation & Management. There are a few glaring obstacles that might limit my overall effectiveness. Things like:

Math and physics
Language skills (I'm pretty good at English, but that's about it.)
My limited capacity to think and care about the whole wide world at the same time
My consistent propensity to fall asleep at night would leave the world hanging

*How are you looking on the Universe Administration qualifications? Just as bad as me? Why or why not?*

Discover how God responds to our rambling:

For my thoughts are not your thoughts, neither are your ways my ways, declares the Lord. For as the heavens are higher than the earth, so are my ways higher than your ways and my thoughts than your thoughts.
**ISAIAH 55:8-9**

We don't understand everything, and God knows that. We have legitimate questions, and He understands. We have to remember what the Bible teaches about the character of God. He is alive, eternal, all-knowing, all-powerful, truthful, holy, majestic, sovereign, righteous, and perfect in all of those ways.

God could have chosen not to create at all. Or, He could have created a world without freedom, so that we were like robots who had to choose His ways.

But He did not. So the questions become: *Will I trust that an infinitely-wise, all-good God chose the plan that would bring the greatest good? Will I believe a perfectly-loving God chose the greatest good, both for His own glory and the greatest good for free creatures?*

I do not speak from blind faith or lack of searching when I tell you that I believe. Will you have faith in the plan God made? Will you trust that His heart toward you is good?

When I have explained something to my children, yet the fullness was still beyond their understanding, it sounded a lot like this:

> *Mommy, I don't understand why I have to have ear surgery.*
> *Oh baby, I have told you all I can. I love you, and I'm doing what's best for you.*
> *Will you trust me?*

> *Mommy, I don't understand why I can't go with my friends.*
> *Oh baby, I have explained all that I can. I love you, so I'm protecting you.*
> *Will you trust me?*

> *Mommy, I don't want to move away from my friends.*
> *Oh baby, I understand your sadness and disappointment. I love you, and I'm doing something good for you. Will you trust me?*

We have a better Father. A better parent. A better truth. Will you trust the One who made you? The One who holds you? The One who loves you? The only One who is qualified and able to do more than you can ask, imagine, or hope? Will you trust His greater purpose in allowing sin and suffering into your life? Will you believe that His steadfast love is wrapped in the sovereignty of His greater thoughts and greater ways?

God wants to redeem everything in our lives:

Our sin natures
Our separation from Him
Our broken hearts
Our suffering
Our pain

Our dysfunctional families
Our minds
Our choices
Our motives

*God has a plan to redeem all that concerns you, and He intends to begin with your heart. Will you receive His offer to redeem? Will you believe in His steadfast love? Or will you spend another year with your arms crossed, muttering to yourself something about how you'd do things differently?*

# READ AND MEDITATE

*TODAY'S READING: PSALMS 25–27*

**MY DAY 10 PRAYER FOR YOU**

*Oh Father God, we need Your plan to redeem our hearts. Our lives. Our families. We need Your steadfast love and mercy. Will You give us a hunger to know You more? Let this dear one begin to see You everywhere she looks. Teach her about the conversation of prayer. Help her to stop making plans so she can follow Your plan. Redeem her suffering. Redeem her mistakes. Redeem her home. Amen.*

# RESPOND IN PRAYER

Return to Psalm 25 and pray those words back to God over your life. Your family. Your struggles. Your sin. Your pain.

_____

_____

_____

_____

_____

_____

_____

_____

_____

_____

DAY 11

# READ, MEDITATE, & PRAY

Remember . . .

The God of peace will soon crush Satan under your feet.
The grace of our Lord Jesus Christ be with you.
**ROMANS 16:20**

## READ AND MEDITATE

*TODAY'S READING: PSALMS 28–30*

**MY DAY 11 PRAYER FOR YOU**

*Father, keep this dear one in the center of Your love. Even in the darkest room. Even in the loneliest places. Even in the mundane routines of her day. Flood her soul with the assurance of Your presence and Your power. Keep singing Your eternal love songs over her. Let her feel what it feels like to be securely loved, and eternally desired. In Your Son's saving name, amen.*

## RESPOND IN PRAYER

Many Christians haven't stopped believing in God, . . . [they are just] living with God at a distance. . . . But as we learn to pray well, we'll discover that this is my Father's world. Because my Father controls everything, I can ask, and He will listen and act.[13]
**PAUL E. MILLER**

DAY 12

# READ, MEDITATE, & PRAY

Twelve days of prayer is such a great start! Hang in there. Keep going, even when it's not pretty, and you can't even think of what to say. Turn toward your Father and go to Him like His child.

## READ AND MEDITATE

*TODAY'S READING: PSALMS 31–33*

**MY DAY 12 PRAYER FOR YOU**

*Father, please give this sweet soul a fresh rest, grace, and peace. Then, down deep inside, will You give new life to her lost passions and dreams? Tell her it's okay to desire everything You made her to desire. Don't let words, disappointments, or pain rob her of the very thing You appointed her to bring into this world. Cheer loudly for her today. Get her attention and turn the volume up so she can hear. Lord, there is no one who can inspire like You. She needs to hear You. Speak through Your Word. Speak to her in prayer. In Jesus' name, amen.*

## RESPOND IN PRAYER

Learning to pray doesn't offer us a less busy life; it offers us a less busy heart. In the midst of outer busyness we can develop an inner quiet.[14]
**PAUL E. MILLER**

_____

_____

_____

_____

_____

_____

_____

_____

_____

# SESSION 3: VIEWER GUIDE

## REDEEMED FOR THE PRAISE OF HIS GLORY

**SOTERIOLOGY:** The study of _____.

**REDEMPTION ACCOMPLISHED:** _____ Christ did to buy redemption for us.

- Soteriology = _____

**REDEMPTION APPLIED:**

- Justification = _____ = _____

- Sanctification = _____ _____

- Glorification = _____ _____

Everyone who calls on the name of the Lord will be saved.
**ROMANS 10:13**

In him we have redemption through his blood, the forgiveness of our trespasses, according to the riches of his grace, which he lavished upon us, in all wisdom and insight making known to us the mystery of his will, according to his purpose, which he set forth in Christ as a plan for the fullness of time, to unite all things in him, things in heaven and things on earth. In him we have obtained an inheritance, having been predestined according to the purpose of him who works all things according to the counsel of his will, so that we who were the first to hope in Christ might be to the praise of his glory. In him you also, when you heard the word of truth, the gospel of your salvation, and believed in him, were sealed with the promised Holy Spirit, who is the guarantee of our inheritance until we acquire possession of it, to the praise of his glory.
**EPHESIANS 1:7-14**

We are redeemed to be the _____ of His _____.

Video sessions available for purchase
at *www.lifeway.com/redeemed*

# WHEN LOVE MAKES A WAY

DAY 13

# WHY IT MATTERS

Hello, blessing!

I'm so excited for you to open your Bible today because I'm praying this is the week lots of lights begin coming on in your heart.

I am not blaming anyone when I tell you I spent too many years not really understanding what I was reading in the Bible. The parables and the stories were so great, but many times I'd find myself in a passage thinking, *I have no idea what they're talking about.* Today is not about calling anybody out. All of us are still learning. I am still learning. But in this study, I'm hoping we get some of the major things in the Bible unwound so we all more easily understand them. It's so much easier to trust and obey the Word of God when the fog begins to lift.

I'm not sure why people try to make things harder than they have to be. Lord knows, I've done it to myself, and I'm desperate not to do that to you here. The Bible can speak so clearly to us at times. Then, we can spend 20 or 30 years adding layers of fuzzy intellect, philosophies, and strategies until we've made the whole thing more complicated than God ever intended it to be.

Jesus' last spoken words in the Book of Matthew instruct us:

> Go therefore and make disciples of all nations, baptizing them in the name of the Father and of the Son and of the Holy Spirit, teaching them to observe all that I have commanded you. And behold, I am with you always, to the end of the age.
> **MATTHEW 28:19-20**

Those precious verses we call the Great Commission are the centerpiece of my life's ambition. At this point, I think I've just about wrestled the search for my "personal ambition" to the mat. All those years ago, I know I clearly heard and understood the Great Commission. Pre-seminary. Pre-speaker girl. Pre-published whatever. That sweet, clear instruction called me to go and teach the Bible, but there have been days I thought my calling had to be more, days when I tried in my own strength to make it more. Through the years, there have been times I've gone the wrong way, stumbled along the way, and listened to so many advisers I didn't know where I was anymore. But I can tell you this about the Lord: if you keep seeking Him, you will find Him.

At some point, I was convinced everybody else was smarter, more educated, and more called than me. Truth is, they probably are all that. Really. But I got turned around, thinking I had to do things the way they did them—go to the places they went—but smart and wise are not always the same thing. You can know lots of smart things yet lack the wisdom to let the plain, main thing be enough. Straight-forward calling lifted straight off a page in the Bible is better for me than a thousand well-meaning conferences, strategies, and workbooks trying to direct me down another foggy path toward purpose.

It also turns out that lots of smart, amazing ideas can make you into a crazy person.

Especially if you are prone to FOMO (fear of missing out). Especially if well-meaning, smart people say, "You oughta _____." Especially if you're not exactly, 100 percent sure and kinda doubt yourself anyway.

But praise God for His faithfulness to keep pursuing the lost! Today, I can answer these questions with strength and clarity from God's Word: What do I want to do with my life? *Make more disciples.* What are my soul's ambitions? *To bear His image. To bring Him joy.*

Disciple-maker. Image-bearer. Joy-bringer. That's who I am.

> *What do you want to do with your life? What is God calling you to do? What are your personal soul ambitions? List a few ideas below.*

This may sound like a stretch to you at first, but I'm absolutely sure it's not. As you and I study the Word of God, meditate on His Word, and spend time in conversation with God, many things in our lives will start to become clear. Like astoundingly, good-grief-that-has-been-staring-at-me-all-this-time kind of clear.

So, on behalf of the Word of God and the Lord of my life, I want to apologize to you if the Scriptures have been misrepresented to you—if clear and simple truth has been made fuzzy. And yet, God, by His grace, still works through whomever He will, however He wills. I wish I'd known God doesn't go foggy on us sooner, but I'm here now. God is good. No time to waste looking in the rearview mirror. I'm too excited about what's ahead to keep looking back. We've got disciples to make!

> *How about you? What areas of your life are covered in the fog of not knowing what to do? Too many options? Lots of opinions?*

*Where are the places in the Bible where you're still not sure what in the world is going on? What the words mean? What it means for your everyday life? Explain.*

*What were your thoughts as you were beginning 40 days of prayer? (A little unnerving because praying feels covered in some kind mysterious fog that always makes you feel like a prayer rookie, maybe even some days even a prayer-dummy?)*

I have intentionally taken us down a different road today. Some days, we just need to remind ourselves why this all matters.

Thy word is a lamp unto my feet and a light unto my path.
**PSALM 119:105**

*Why do we need to understand what it means to be redeemed?*

*If you had to choose one, what would you say is the most common personal struggle affecting women in our culture?*

*What about the most common personal struggle for Christian women?*

Maybe you said the same thing for each, or maybe not. We may have vastly different opinions about women's personal struggles and that's okay; this isn't a debate. Yet I believe one of the greatest struggles women face is the everyday battle with insecurity.

*Jot down some of the ways insecurity affects our lives.*

*In friendship:*

*As a wife:*

*As a mom:*

*In the workplace:*

*At church:*

*In our communities:*

Insecurity has woven a weakness through everything. Breeding more insecurity is the high aim of Satan, and right now on the planet, he's doing a pretty good job. There are probably a million diverse reasons and ways a woman can become insecure, but true healing and strength will only begin in one way. It must begin in the soul—in exactly the place Jesus wants to come and live, come and heal, come and restore, come and empower, come and bless.

If we do not believe in Jesus, that soul work has not begun.

If we do not know what it means to believe, what happens when we believe, or who we are because we believe, we are still living from insecurity, not the strength Christ bought for us on the cross.

Do you see the difference it makes to know and understand these truths?

The woman who knows what it means to be redeemed lives an entirely different life than the one who isn't sure. In a word, she is secure. She knows who she was, what happened when she entrusted her life to Jesus, and who she is becoming because she follows Him.

She is redeemed, and she is being redeemed. And in heaven, she will be finally, fully redeemed.

> She is forgiven.
> She belongs to God.
> She is filled with the Holy Spirit.
> She is being changed by His power and His grace.
> She has access to God in prayer.
> She is on her way home.

> **Whatever we do, we must not treat The Great Commission like it's The Great Suggestion.**[1]
> **CHARLES R. SWINDOLL**

In Matthew 28, it's the redeemed who go and tell others about the Redeemer. They tell with their voices and with their lives. You cannot tell what you do not understand, and we will not obey Jesus' strong "Go" command if we aren't really sure what to say.

We've gone off-road today because I wanted to remind you that knowing—and believing—these truths can radically change your life. And when that kind of woman goes and tells others, well, that's exactly how the disciples turned this world upside down.

# READ AND MEDITATE

## TODAY'S READING: PSALMS 34–36

### MY DAY 13 PRAYER FOR YOU

*Oh Father, teach us about redeemed so we can tell others. Teach us about redeemed so we can live as the redeemed. Help this dear one lean in toward Your voice, unclench her fists, and cooperate with the Holy Spirit. Will You bless her, Lord? Bless her studies, her prayers, her honesty, and her heart. Tell her over and over that You are with her always—always and always, even until the end of the age. Oh thank You, Jesus, amen.*

# RESPOND IN PRAYER

I'm not going to try and convince you that you ought to pray. If the struggles of those you love, and the heartache of the world, or your own dreams, desires, and afflictions do not move you, nothing I say . . . would be more compelling.[2]
**JOHN ELDRIDGE**

**DAY 14**

# WAITING FOR REDEMPTION

Yesterday's study was about the Great Commission. Jesus gave the Great Commission to all who believe in Him.

In order to make more disciples, we've got to know what we believe. If you happen to be a mom, then boom, you already have disciples to make. Even if you're not a mom, most of us don't have to look very far. God usually has a small group of disciples already gathered around, staring right back at us, just waiting for us to grow in our faith and get on with it!

*Has God already given you a small group of people who need to be discipled and taught? Are they in your home? At your work? Live on your street? Your dorm? Play on your team? List them.*

*What if God isn't asking you to become a Bible professor? How would you respond if He's just asking you to teach someone else what you've been learning about Him?*

> There must be knowledge of God before there can be love to God: there must be a knowledge of divine things, as they are revealed, before there can be an enjoyment of them. We must try to make out, as far as our finite mind can grasp it, what God means by this and what he means by that; otherwise we may kiss the book and have no love to its contents, we may reverence the letter and yet really have no devotion towards the Lord who speaks to us in these words.[3]
> C.H. SPURGEON

## BEING REDEEMED IN THE OLD TESTAMENT (NOT AS BORING AS IT SOUNDS!)

If I say, "Old Testament," do you say, "I think I have some laundry to do?" If I promise this won't take long or be painful, will you hang with me? Honestly, I tried to breeze over this part because I didn't want to scare you away, but if Jesus is the solution, we've got to go back and understand the problem a little better. Get the words right. Understand their meaning a little better. I think taking the time to go step-by-step is going to be so helpful.

Sometimes, it's tempting to try and interpret the Bible based on our own experiences, but here, with redeemed being the most central idea in all Christianity, I want to caution you to keep the Bible as your source for right understanding. There is nothing in all of human experience that comes close to being "like" what Jesus endured and accomplished so that we can be redeemed. We have no analogy or story that compares to His sacrifice for us.

Maybe that's why some of us don't have a good handle on these terms and ideas. We know we need to be redeemed, but how God accomplished our redemption is something we just don't think about every day.

Now, here is where we are going to fly through the entire Old Testament concerning redemption. But first, to every diligent Bible professor and scholar, I want to ask your forgiveness in advance. The whole Bible is about Jesus and God's plan to redeem His people. No one should zoom through the Old Testament, and I know that, but we only have 40 days together, and redeemed lives are the main thing, so we've gotta roll!

*Immediately after the fall, God announced His plan to provide salvation for all humankind. Can you remember the verse in Genesis where He made that promise? (Hint: We spent most of last week talking about it.)*

*Genesis 3: _____*

After God's promise, the rest of the Old Testament prepares for the coming of Jesus, who will bring salvation and restore humanity to God. You could divide the books of the Old Testament by their purpose like this:

**GENESIS TO DEUTERONOMY:** The books of the law; lay the foundation for the need for Christ.

**JOSHUA TO NEHEMIAH:** The historical books; Israel enters the Holy Land to eventually produce the Holy One.

**JOB TO SONG OF SOLOMON:** The poetic books; expressed the longing for Christ.

**ISAIAH TO MALACHI:** The prophetic books; proclaimed an expectation for Christ.[4]

Last week we mentioned in the OT (Old Testament) that God made covenant promises to redeem His people. God made those covenant promises to His people not because they deserved His promise, but because of His unlimited grace and steadfast love.

Sometimes, you'll hear people talk about the OT and focus mainly on the wrath of God— and His wrath over sin is certainly evident—but in doing so, they can miss the grace of God woven through every page.

*Missing the grace of God is easy to do sometimes, so let's stop right here and practice. List three gifts of God's grace to you today. Try to write these off the top of your head. Simple is better.*

Next up, we have a few OT terms to look at. Even though we're just skimming the surface of their meaning, I think this is going to be really helpful.

## THE OLD TESTAMENT LAW

Through Moses, God gave the law to those who believed in Him. There were mainly three kinds of law:

**JUDICIAL LAW:** governed the disputes of the Israelite people and maintained justice

**CEREMONIAL LAW:** dealt with the procedures and sacrifices required for worship and forgiveness

**MORAL LAW:** based on the character of God, for all who believe in God[5]

> For by works of the law no human being will be justified in his sight, since through the law comes knowledge of sin.
> **ROMANS 3:20**

*According to Romans 3:20, what was the purpose of the law?*

*By establishing God's requirements for living, the law revealed the great sinfulness of man. Not sure if the law reveals your sinfulness? Take a look at the Mosaic law in Exodus 20:1-18. How did you stack up? Are you a perfect law-keeper or how did the law reveal your sin?*

*Now, read Galatians 2:16. Can someone be saved by keeping the law? Why or why not?*

The law was never intended to save anyone. The law was given to make us conscious of our sin. The OT way of salvation was always through grace alone, by faith alone, in Christ alone. God's grace to man required faith for man to believe that God would send the promised Messiah.

*Read Romans 4:3 and Genesis 15:6. How was Abraham made righteous?*

*How were people saved before Jesus came?*

The requirement for salvation has always been faith.

*Now, read Matthew 5:17-18. Who fulfilled the law?*

## OLD TESTAMENT SACRIFICES

Under the law, God required animal sacrifices as a temporary covering of sins. Sacrifices were a temporary way to atone and be cleansed of sin. An OT sinner had to atone endlessly to be cleansed of sin.

*Read Hebrews 10:1-4. What does this passage say about animal sacrifices and their ability to save? Explain.*

The purpose of OT sacrifice was:

1. To acknowledge the holiness of God
2. To show the seriousness of sin
3. To provide a temporary forgiveness of sin for those who believed in God
4. To point to the coming sacrifice of Jesus Christ.

The OT sacrifices were like a placeholder to be maintained while the people of God waited for the Messiah.

## THE OLD TESTAMENT DAY OF ATONEMENT

> Now on the tenth day of this seventh month is the Day of Atonement. It shall be for you a time of holy convocation, and you shall afflict yourselves and present a food offering to the LORD. And you shall not do any work on that very day, for it is a Day of Atonement, to make atonement for you before the LORD your God.
> **LEVITICUS 23:27-28**

Also known as Yom Kippur, the Day of Atonement continues to be the most solemn holy day for Jews. The ceremony of rituals was established by God to atone for the unintentional sins of the people. The full ceremony is described in Leviticus 16.

- Before entering the tabernacle, the priest (Aaron) was washed and bathed, then dressed in special garments.
- The priest sacrificed a bull as a sin offering for himself and his family, placing blood on the altar.
- Then, the priest sacrificed a goat for the sins of the people, placing blood on the altar.
- A second goat was used as a "scapegoat." Aaron placed his hands on its head and confessed the rebellion of Israel. The goat was then sent into the wilderness to carry away the sins of the people.
- The people were forgiven for another year.

Observing the Day of Atonement ended for Christians with the death of Jesus Christ when He served as the final, forever atonement for the sin of humanity.

> For Christ has entered, not into holy places made with hands, which are copies of the true things, but into heaven itself, now to appear in the presence of God on our behalf. Nor was it to offer himself repeatedly, as the high priest enters the holy places every year with blood not his own, for then he would have had to suffer repeatedly since the foundation of the world. But as it is, he has appeared once for all at the end of the ages to put away sin by the sacrifice of himself.
> **HEBREWS 9:24-26**

## PREPARING FOR THE REDEEMER

The Old Testament was preparing us to understand the meaning of Christ's death in the New Testament. Here are some of the things we just learned:

- Anyone who sins is deemed guilty.
- Guilt must be punished as an offense to the holiness of God.

- God determined that the guilty can only come to Him in a very specific way called the law.
- A life must be sacrificed to atone for sin.
- The sacrifice deals with guilt so that God extends forgiveness.
- Faith is required to accept God's specific ways.
- Faith is required to receive His promised forgiveness.

I hope that wherever you're sitting right now, the all-surpassing beauty of God's Word is becoming even sweeter to you. I hope some of the words we use in our faith are becoming a little easier to understand. The Bible you hold in your hands is so powerfully and intricately written. The more I study, the more in awe I become.

# READ AND MEDITATE

*TODAY'S READING: PSALMS 37–39*

**MY DAY 14 PRAYER FOR YOU**

*Father, I pray for awe. For jaw-dropping, this-is-all-coming-together-and-starting-to-make-sense kind of awe. Lord, give us the grace to trust Your ways. To humble ourselves at Your holiness. To trust in the way You choose to deal with sin. To honor Your thoughts as higher. To respect Your ways as above our own. And every place we lack faith, will You add Yours? Will You send the Holy Spirit to explain more deeply? Will You help me explain who You are to someone who doesn't know You? Because Jesus became the perfect sacrifice for sin, I am grateful to pray in His name, amen.*

# RESPOND IN PRAYER

I have come to see prayer as a privilege, not a duty. Like all good things, prayer requires some discipline. Yet I believe that life with God should seem more like friendship than duty. Prayer includes moments of ecstasy and also dullness, mindless distraction and acute concentration, flashes of joy and bouts of irritation. In other words, prayer has features in common with all relationships that matter.[6]
**PHILIP YANCEY**

DAY 15

# JESUS IS THE WAY

Every day while I've been writing this study, an angst comes over me. I don't want this study to feel like a seminary class to you. I'm desperate for these truths not to become boring or stale. And every day, I come to the same conclusion: God must be the One to bring these truths alive in your soul. I have to trust Him with His Word and His work.

I can't manipulate one thing or make you have a passionate relationship with God. I can't beg you to pray or force you to read through the Psalms. I can only hope to guide you as I'm able. To communicate my passion for the Bible. To tell you how God has applied His Word to my life. And then believe the Holy Spirit will bring you something personal and greater.

Today, I'm praying you get one main thing. It's the most important thing. It's the one thing that changes everything:

**Jesus is the way.**

He is the only way to forgiveness. The only way to be restored to God. The only way to eternal life.

Jesus is the only answer for this fallen world. He is our only victory against evil. He is our only peace. Our only joy. Our only hope.

But in order to fully understand that Jesus is the only way, we have to finally realize we are not the way.

> We cannot undo the sin nature we inherited.
> We cannot find our own way to satisfy God's holy demands.
> We cannot perfectly keep the law.
> We cannot claim to be a spotless sacrifice.

But, hey, we're not all bad people. A lot of us are actually pretty good people. We've tried to do the right things, be nice to people, and help people when we can. Goodness, we're not all big, fat sinners. We're more like little ol' white lie sinners—with an occasional mistake. But really, that doesn't happen very much.

Here's the thing lots of good people miss: The Bible says all have sinned. And just a little bit of sin separates you from God.

The separated need a way back to God.

### Jesus is the way.

As you know, the New Testament opens with the fulfillment of prophecy. The long awaited Messiah was born. Turn to John 1:29 and fill in the blank:

> *Behold, _____ _____ _____ _____, who takes away the sin of the world!*

My seminary professor wrote about the coming of Christ: "the anticipation of the Old Testament became the realization of the New."[7] Jesus quoted the Psalms when He declared the reason for His coming,

> Then I said, "Behold, I have come to do your will, O God,
> as it is written of me in the scroll of the book."
> **HEBREWS 10:7**

There is no way I could have made this happen. I've moved the order of this study around so much, I can hardly keep up with myself, but I just scrolled down to look at our reading for today in the Psalms, and there was the passage Jesus recalled.

> *You'll read the whole chapter later, but for now, turn to Psalm 40:6-8. It was spoken by David and later referred to by Jesus. It's important enough for us to stop for a minute and consider for ourselves. Write out Psalm 40:8 below as a personal prayer.*

Ever since Genesis 3:15, Jesus had been the promised way back to God. The Old Testament sacrifices were temporary and were not able to clear the sinner's conscience.

> According to this arrangement, gifts and sacrifices are offered
> that cannot perfect the conscience of the worshiper.
> **HEBREWS 9:9b**

So, Jesus willingly came to earth as a man in order to become both the priest who offers an atoning sacrifice *and* the sacrifice itself.

Does that get to you the way it does me? No OT priest was ever clean enough. No OT sacrifice was ever pure enough. So Christ became both for us.

*Turn to Hebrews 2:17 and fill in the blank below.*

*Therefore he had to be made like his brothers in every respect, so that he might become a merciful and faithful high priest in the service of God, to make _____ for the sins of the people.*

Depending on the Bible translation you are reading, maybe you wrote the words *propitiation, reconciliation,* or *atonement.* Depending on your faith journey, you may or may not understand what you just wrote down.

*Atonement* is one of those words we can hear and read without actually understanding what it means. Or, if you're like me, for a long time I would have said, *I kinda know what it means. Sorta. Maybe. But don't ask me to write it down or anything.*

*Propitiation.* Are you kidding? I don't know three people who could give me a quick definition much better than, *I think it's a Bible word.*

Here are some of the Bible words that refer to the *solution for sin:*

**ATONEMENT:** means to repair a wrong done. In the Bible, this is the broader term referring to Christ's death that removed our guilt from sin.

**PROPITIATION:** means turning away anger by the offering of a gift. In the Bible, propitiation focuses on God's wrath being turned away by Jesus' death on the cross.

**EXPIATION:** means the act of making amends. In the Bible, expiation focuses on the removal of human sin and guilt.

Christ's sacrifice both propitiates (turns away) the wrath of God and expiates (covers) human sin.[8] The atonement is everything Christ did so that sinners can be redeemed.

## Atonement Truth at a Glance

- **The holiness and justice of God demanded a price be paid for sin.**

- **The death and resurrection of Jesus completely atoned (made repair) for the sin of man.**

- **The atonement paid the price in full.**

- **Redemption (reconciliation) between God and man was fully accomplished by the atonement of Christ.**

*Here are some more truths about atonement. Circle the key phrases or main words in each.*

☐ *The atonement was God's action to repair the broken relationship that sin caused between man and God.*

☐ *The atonement was initiated by God, through His Son, Jesus Christ. Mankind had nothing to do with it.*

☐ *When Jesus atoned for the sin of mankind through His death and resurrection, redemption was bought. The transaction is complete.*

☐ *There was only one atonement, when Christ endured the judgment for our sins, and there will never need to be another (Heb. 9:26).*

*Now, read Galatians 4:4-7. When did this event happen?*

*Who was the sender?*

*How did the Son come?*

*What was His purpose?*

*What do the redeemed receive?*

I love the story of a man who was asked, "How long have you been redeemed?" His answer gives such perspective to this great Bible truth. The man reportedly responded, "I was redeemed by Jesus Christ more than 2,000 years ago when He gave His life to atone for my sin. But I only found out about a year ago."

Remember this: Redemption was accomplished by the atonement. It is finished. The full price of redemption has been paid.

**Jesus is the way.**

# READ AND MEDITATE

*TODAY'S READING: PSALMS 40–42*

## MY DAY 15 PRAYER FOR YOU

*Father, there is nothing to do but worship You. Praise You. Rejoice over You. Sing Your praises. Draw close to You. Run to You. Thank You, and thank You, and thank You. The depth of Your love we cannot reach. The grace of Your forgiveness we cannot understand. You are good. You are holy. There is none like You. In the saving name of Jesus, amen.*

# RESPOND IN PRAYER

The glory of the cross is bound up with the effectiveness of its accomplishment.[9]
**JOHN MURRAY**

**More of those Bible Words**

- *Substitutionary Atonement:* Jesus died in our place, acting as our substitute, receiving the punishment for our sins.

- *Restoration:* Jesus' death repaired (restored) the relationship between God and man.

- *Ransom:* The justice of God required payment for the offense of sin. Jesus paid our ransom and freed us from debt.

**DAY 16**

# BECOMING REDEEMED

I do realize that for many of you, this is the first "Bible study" you've ever done. I'm excited because I know you're getting the "main, plain Bible thing," but I also realize you've got an everyday life going on. You need God to show up and show off and do some God-sized work in your life. This afternoon!

Honestly, I believe He will, and I believe, if you look around, you'll recognize that He is already at work in your life.

As you get to know Him better, God promises to bless your diligence to seek Him.

> Blessed are those who keep his testimonies, who seek him with their whole heart.
> **PSALM 119:2**

God does not pitch out His blessings to those who are far off. Instead, His blessings are reserved for those who draw near. His story was important enough for Him to preserve for us all these years. He wants you and me to understand His history and His glory and His ways. He wants us to know Him—and His Son.

He wants our lives to tell His story. The redeemed story.

And so here we are, each one of us faced with a decision to make. Will your life tell His story? Will your life sing the song of the redeemed?

# THE REDEEMED STORY

Below you'll see that I've tried to lay out the theology of atonement in the simplest, most easy to understand way.

## WHAT HAPPENED?

Man caused the broken relationship with God—guilty (Isa. 53:6a; 59:12).

The death sentence was imposed—for eternity (Rev. 21:8).

The honor and justice of God's character was offended by sin—our debt (Jer. 50:29).

The nature of man became enslaved to sin—chained and shackled (John 8:34-36).

## THE AWFUL STATE OF MAN

Man could not undo what had been done—hopeless (Rom. 3:23).

Man could not avoid the penalty of death—condemned (Rom. 6:23).

Man could not become good enough to overcome sin—his debt could not be paid (Gal. 2:16).

The shackles of sin could not be broken (Rom. 6:16).

## THE CHOICE GOD MADE

God could have just walked away. Game over. Disobedience – Done. But He did not (Deut. 7:9).

God is holy and just. And yet, God is Steadfast Love (Ps. 107).

God made a way for man to be restored (2 Cor. 5:19).

There was no other way to restore, except to satisfy the debt (Col. 2:14), defeat the certainty of death (2 Tim. 1:10), and break the shackles of sin (Ps. 107:14).

And no one else could do that except God Himself (Acts 4:12).

So He did (Rom. 8:3).

God sent His only Son, Jesus, so that whoever believes in Him can be saved (John 3:16).

Jesus is the way (John 14:6).

Those who believe in Jesus will be saved from the penalty of their sins. They will be redeemed (John 3:36).

Being redeemed is being restored to relationship with God (Gal. 4:4-7).

Did you catch that? A perfectly Holy God could have just walked away, mumbling, *You freely chose what you got, so I'm outta here.*

But God did not walk away because He is also Steadfast Love. Steadfast Love sent His Son to redeem.

More importantly, today you need to know Steadfast Love sent His Son, so that you can be redeemed—so your life will be redeemed.

## BECOMING REDEEMED

I hope the very personal reality of God's love for you is sinking deeper and deeper into your heart. But I also know the heart can become hardened by this world. Honestly, without a relationship with God, a hard heart is just about the only way to survive some days. It's the only way most people survive.

Some of you need to decide if you believe what we've been studying these past two and a half weeks. Some of you need to return to the truth you already believed. Here's the deal: God's love for you is so personal that no one can believe for you, except you. No one gets to believe on a group pass. You are too precious to God. His Steadfast Love will not be watered down or doled out like stadium seats. It is the unchanging desire of your Father in heaven that you be restored to His love. He is personally inviting you back to relationship with Him. You are the only one who can respond for you.

Sometimes you might hear someone ask, "Will you receive God's gift of eternal life? Will you receive Jesus? Will you receive forgiveness of your sins?" What they mean is Jesus bought the gift of being redeemed, but His redemption is not yours until you receive it.

> Then he brought them out and said, "Sirs, what must I do to be saved?" And they said, "Believe in the Lord Jesus, and you will be saved, you and your household." And they spoke the word of the Lord to him and to all who were in his house. And he took them the same hour of the night and washed their wounds; and he was baptized at once, he and all his family. Then he brought them up into his house and set food before them. And he rejoiced along with his entire household that he had believed in God.
> **ACTS 16:30-34**

*How does Acts 16:30-34 say we receive redemption?*

We are redeemed when we believe in Jesus. Because believing is such a big deal, we're going to spend tomorrow learning what it really means to believe.

Maybe I spent too many years doubting whether or not I had "believed right" or "believed enough," but I'm bound and determined that under my teaching you will not have questions about what it means to believe in Jesus.

It's not even that hard. And it's not complicated. There are no hoops to jump through. So, tomorrow we'll take a day to settle the truth of believing, once and for all.

I love you so much. I am praying for you all the time. I am begging God to redeem.

# READ AND MEDITATE

*TODAY'S READING: PSALMS 43–45*

**MY DAY 16 PRAYER FOR YOU**

*Sweet Lord, my Savior and my friend, Jesus. Do not allow anything I say to complicate the most beautiful truth in Scripture. Give this dear one Your grace to read, to receive, to believe. Teach her Yourself through the power of the Holy Spirit. Give her the words she needs to tell others about You. Settle her heart and encourage her with Your presence. As she reads through the psalms today, bless her. Shout to her. Keep teaching her to pray. In Jesus' name, amen.*

# RESPOND IN PRAYER

"Be still and know that I am God": the Latin imperative for "be still" is vacate. As Simon Tugwell explains, "God invites us to take a holiday [vacation], to stop being God for awhile, and let him be God" . . . "We can stop doing all those important things we have to do in our capacity as God, and leave it to him to be God." Prayer allows me to admit my failures, weaknesses, and limitations to One who responds to human vulnerability with infinite mercy.[10]
**PHILIP YANCEY**

**DAY 17**

# WHEN YOU BELIEVE

Did you know that before you even give one thought to believing in Jesus, God is calling you to Himself? Jesus said,

> To him the gatekeeper opens. The sheep hear his voice,
> and he calls his own sheep by name and leads them out.
> **JOHN 10:3**

*How does Jesus call us?*

He calls us by name. Haley. Sarah. Ashley. Taylor. Morgan. Lisa. Carol. Jessica. AnnaDell. Brittany. Jennifer. Emily. Nicole. Rachel. Michelle. Tiffany. Caitlin. Amy. Amanda. Jordan. Paige. Katherine. Kelly. Anna Grace. Gail. Faye. Molly Claire. Bethany. Maria. April.

God knows who you are, what you are, and where you are. And when God calls you, the call is so very personal, you recognize He is speaking to you.

Exactly, what is God calling you to? He is calling you back into relationship with Him. Can you let that sink in for a minute?

> God is not calling you to condemnation.
> God is not calling you to boring.
> God is not calling you to ignorance.

This is a relationship, and God is calling you into the intimacy of an embrace. An embrace is mutual and never one-sided, or it's not an embrace.

The truth of God's steadfast love will require you to embrace it by faith.

Let's take the time to talk about what it means when someone believes in Jesus.

But to all who did receive him, who believed in his name,
he gave the right to become children of God.
**JOHN 1:12**

In this study, we aren't pulling out the original Greek language very often, but here, I think it's valuable for us to read and comprehend. The Greek word for "believe" is πιστεύω, pisteúō, which means:

- to believe, have faith in, trust[11]
- to believe to the extent of complete trust and reliance—"to believe in"[12]
- one believes, he continues to believe, for he has eternal life in him[13]
- to entrust, commit in trust to someone . . . to have something committed to one's trust or charge.[14]

Many people on this earth believe Jesus was a real man. And many believe Jesus was the Son of God. Still more believe Jesus was crucified on a cross to bear punishment for the sins of the world. They "believe" a lot about Jesus, but their version of believing is more like an acknowledgment of facts or being in agreement with a report. But the Greek definition, and the Bible's intended use, means there is more to believing than just agreeing.

Let me see if I can illustrate. Here in North Carolina, there is a place called Grandfather Mountain. At the top of Grandfather Mountain, there is a bridge called the Mile High Swinging Bridge. It's called *mile high* because the elevation there is more than a mile high. It's called *swinging* because the suspension allows the bridge to swing between the tops of the mountain. And everything makes that bridge swing. A little breeze. A big wind. Dorky teenagers fast-walking beside you. I've been there with my family, and it's the kind of thing that makes you ask, *Why? Why was this necessary? And why are we here? And why are all these other people here?* Honestly, it's just awful.

At the place where you step onto the bridge, there is a fairly large "holding area." No one asks you to wait before you cross, people just hold up there anyway. They hold because they are like me—instantly sick to death about the whole idea. They realize, if you go over, there is only one way back.

Everyone standing around me believed the bridge would hold them. We saw the bridge holding other people. We read every single word about the history of the bridge. The construction methods. The engineering science of suspension bridges. And the most recent inspection notice by the state of North Carolina. We believed the bridge was safe and sturdy, but that is not the kind of believing the Bible speaks of regarding Jesus. The Greek word for *believe* requires more. In the Bible, to believe in Jesus means to entrust your life to His truth. At the bridge, it meant stepping out, onto the thing I believed would hold me. And praise God, it did.

To believe in Jesus requires all these things:
knowledge + conviction + trust. All of these things together = FAITH.

*Turn to Hebrews 11:1 to fill in the following.*

*Now faith is the _____ of things _____*
*_____, the conviction of things not seen.*

Back to our bridge illustration.

**KNOWLEDGE:** I knew of the bridge and its history of holding strong since 1952.

**CONVICTION:** I became convinced that the bridge would certainly hold me up.

**TRUST:** I took the first step, out from my holding place and onto the bridge.

**Faith is not the act of God; it is not God who believes in Christ for salvation, it is the sinner. It is by God's grace that a person is able to believe but faith is an activity on the part of the person and of him alone. In faith *we* receive and rest upon Christ alone for salvation.**

**Faith is a whole-souled movement of self-commitment to Christ for salvation from sin and its consequences.**[15]
**JOHN MURRAY**

As a Bible teacher, I can't tell you that having faith in God is anything like putting your faith in a mile-high swinging bridge. I'm going to blow our theology to pieces if I do that. But truth is, some days having faith in God feels a whole lot like stepping out onto that bridge.

There wasn't one thing pretty about the way I walked across the Mile High Swinging Bridge that day. I had tears in my eyes. I was clutching the steel side rails for dear life. I could feel my knees shaking. Everything in me wanted to scream every time someone went past me and made my part of the bridge swing. And some days, there is nothing pretty about our faith either.

I hear you saying, "But you can see a bridge right in front of you and you can't see God." To which I'd like to offer, it wasn't the things I could see that I was worried about. It was always the unseen. A loose cable. Unseen cracks. A gust of wind.

In much the same way, we stand on the seashore watching a sunset display the splendor of God's glory. We meet people who have trusted God before us, and we can see with our eyes the transforming power of God in their lives. We hear in our spirit the still, small voice of God calling us back to Himself. But to embrace this God will require us to believe. To have faith.

Exactly what is God asking you to believe? He is asking you to believe that in Jesus you can be saved from the penalty of your sin.

We've worked really hard to get to this very place. If something in the phrase above still doesn't make sense to you, that's okay. Go back through the previous pages. Maybe you skipped a day or there was something that just didn't take hold. I really want you to know what God is asking you to believe—and to know some of the sweetest Bible verses:

> For God so loved the world, that he gave his only Son, that whoever believes in him should not perish but have eternal life.
> JOHN 3:16

> For "everyone who calls on the name of the Lord will be saved."
> ROMANS 10:13

> Everyone who believes that Jesus is the Christ has been born of God, and everyone who loves the Father loves whoever has been born of him.
> 1 JOHN 5:1

*From the verses above, exactly who is God inviting to believe?*

That's right: Whoever. Everyone. Whosoever. Any. All. The world.

And one last thing, exactly how do we tell God we believe?

> If you confess with your mouth that Jesus is Lord and believe in your heart that God raised him from the dead, you will be saved. For with the heart one believes and is justified, and with the mouth one confesses and is saved. For the Scripture says, "Everyone who believes in him will not be put to shame." For there is no distinction between Jew and Greek; for the same Lord is Lord of all, bestowing his riches on all who call on him.
> ROMANS 10:9-12

To "confess with your mouth" is to openly express your allegiance. To say. To tell. To pray. So, can you do this part wrong? Let me be clear with you. No. The only requirement for believing is faith.

The only way to do this wrong is to pretend. Or say words you don't yet believe. Or just go along with a crowd. Or pray a prayer you don't mean. The only way not to believe "correctly" is to not believe.

Do you remember the father in Mark 9? He brought his son to Jesus to be healed. Jesus said, "All things are possible for one who believes" (Mark 9:23). Then the father immediately shouted to Jesus, some of the most honest words ever spoken, "I believe; help my unbelief!" (v. 24). The father was essentially saying,

I believe You as much as I can. Help me believe You more than I know how.
I believe everything I know about You, but I'm suddenly struck that I don't
  know very much at all.
I believe You, but it doesn't feel like enough because the Son of God deserves
  more than this.
I believe You, but my words sound so small. Please help me believe You more.
  Help me really believe You!

And here's what we know. In response to the father's honest cries, Jesus healed the son. No sermons about believing Him for bigger things. No, *Come back when you get your believing sorted out.* No doubts cast about the certainty of his belief. Or whether or not the man used exactly the right words to speak his belief.

The father believed with all the faith he had, and it was enough.

*Today, do you believe what Christ has accomplished for you?*

But to all who did receive him, who believed in his name,
he gave the right to become children of God.
**JOHN 1:12**

*Write your name in the blanks below.*

*Jesus redeemed _____ with His life.*

*Jesus restored _____ to full relationship with God.*

*Jesus did what _____ could not do.*

*It's done. It is finished. _____ is redeemed.*

# READ AND MEDITATE

We have thought on your steadfast love, O God, in the midst of your temple.
**PSALM 48:9**

*TODAY'S READING: PSALMS 46—48*

**MY DAY 17 PRAYER FOR YOU**

*Father, I pray for my sister the grace to believe what You have accomplished for her. And then the grace to believe You more. That belief in Your gift of redemption will become a lifetime of living as Your redeemed. Father, make her spiritual foundation strong and steady. Sturdy every weak place in her soul. Settle her doubts and relieve her fears. Bless this sweet believer in Jesus' name, amen.*

# RESPOND IN PRAYER

The Holy Scriptures are our letters from home.[17]
**AUGUSTINE OF HIPPO**

DAY 18

# READ, MEDITATE, & PRAY

Remember, when you believe in Jesus, His Redemption Accomplished becomes your Redemption Applied. The gift Christ bought becomes yours. You are redeemed.

## READ AND MEDITATE

*TODAY'S READING: PSALMS 49–51*

**MY DAY 18 PRAYER FOR YOU**

*Father, stamp REDEEMED on the heart of this one. Give her a new joy. Renewed passion. The freedom to celebrate this truth in her life. Bring fresh light into her eyes. New peace in her heart. Lift her out of that weary place where she has lived and sing over her Your songs of love. Your songs of rest. Your songs of hope. Bless this redeemed soul. In the Savior's name, amen.*

## RESPOND IN PRAYER

I had then, and at other times, the greatest delight in the holy Scriptures, of any book whatsoever. Oftentimes in reading it, every word seemed to touch my heart. I felt a harmony between something in my heart, and those sweet powerful words. I seemed often to see so much light, exhibited by every sentence, and such a refreshing ravishing food communicated, that I could not get along in reading. Used oftentimes to dwell long on one sentence, to see the wonders contained in it; and yet almost every sentence seemed to be full of wonders.[18]
**JONATHAN EDWARDS**

DAY 19

# READ, MEDITATE, & PRAY

Remember: Jesus, our Redeemer. Jesus came to atone for the sin of mankind.

He died in our place, acting as our substitute, taking the punishment for our sins.
His death repaired (restored) the relationship between God and man by dealing with sin.
His death bought us back (redeemed) from slavery to sin.
His death bought us back (redeemed) from the penalty of sin.
His death bought us back (redeemed) from the shame of sin.

## READ AND MEDITATE

*TODAY'S READING: PSALMS 52–54*

**MY DAY 19 PRAYER FOR YOU**

*Father, let us pray the sweet prayers of the redeemed. Honest. Like a child. Secure. Needy. And add to her prayers an even greater faith in Your love. Help her to believe, and then, believe You more. In Jesus' powerful name, amen.*

## RESPOND IN PRAYER

Prayer is . . . doubt's destroyer, ruin's remedy, the antidote to all anxieties.[19]
**C.H. SPURGEON**

_____

_____

_____

_____

_____

_____

_____

_____

_____

_____

# SESSION 4: VIEWER GUIDE

## REDEEMED FOR GRACE

Everyone who calls on the name of the Lord will be saved.
**ROMANS 10:13**

But God, being rich in mercy, because of the great love with which he loved
us, even when we were dead in our trespasses, made us alive together with
Christ—by grace you have been saved—and raised us up with him and seated
us with him in the heavenly places in Christ Jesus, so that in the coming
ages he might show the immeasurable riches of his grace in kindness toward
us in Christ Jesus. For by grace you have been saved through faith. And this
is not your own doing; it is the gift of God, not a result of works, so that no
one may boast. For we are his workmanship, created in Christ Jesus for good
works, which God prepared beforehand, that we should walk in them.
**EPHESIANS 2:4-10**

**GRACE COMES TO US IN THREE WAYS:**

1. We are by _____ grace.

2. The Lord is calling us to _____ it.

3. We have been given _____ _____ by the
   hand of God.

Video sessions available for purchase
at *www.lifeway.com/redeemed*

WHEN LOVE CHANGES YOU

DAY 20

# YOUR STORY, SO FAR

Sometimes, it only takes a few words to communicate half a lifetime.

> *I grew up military.*
> *My parents are divorced.*
> *I was raised on a farm.*
> *I am an only child.*

My few words are these: *I was born into a long line of storytellers.* Now you need to understand, I'm not talking about your C.S. Lewis kind of storyteller. We're more of the Blue Ridge Mountain kind. Front porch sitters. Cackle into the night kind of tellers. The funniest people you've never met. Comedians, every one of us. We may not have been the smartest bunch on the street, but if you stopped by, there was going to be story. And if all was right with the world, there'd be the laugher that makes you cry tears at the end. I'm not saying we didn't have hard things, because there were plenty. I'm just saying that story walked us through. And story helped us heal.

Last fall, I attended a conference all about story. I signed up for the conference to continue learning how to tell a better story. Story is my sweet spot, after all. My jam. My heritage.

My take away from that conference? God wanted me to learn how to *live* a better story.

That is the assignment of the redeemed. But, there will be no better story for our lives until our story is lived inside the greater story of God. The greater story is not about us. It's all about God. He is the Author and the Main Character, and with every turn of the page, from beginning to end, God is the hero. He doesn't want us to just write Him into our story somewhere along the way. He wants us to sit with Him and learn from Him, so that His story begins rewriting ours.

> *Turn to Ephesians 1:3-14. This beautiful passage takes us from eternity to eternity. Verses 6,12, and 14 tell us why God chooses to redeem us. According to those verses, what is the motivation of God to redeem?*

## THE REDEEMED SAY SO

*Psalm 107 celebrates redeemed stories. Read through the first 22 verses and note any phrases that apply to your own journey with God.*

In the back of our conference notebook, we were left with these words,

**I believe it's true every person should write their memoir if for no other reason than it helps them understand who they are, what's happened to them and who it is their lives have caused them to become. A person who understands themselves is easier to connect with, more settled and, most importantly, can see how their story interconnects with the stories of others.[1]**

It's important for the redeemed to know where they have been, what God has done, and who they are becoming because of His love. Then, the redeemed glorify the One who saves them by connecting their stories to others. The redeemed say so by telling the world the story of what God has done.

Sometimes, we don't have very much to say because we haven't taken the time to remember. Let's spend the rest of our time today remembering and recording your story, so far.

## YOUR STORY, SO FAR

Even if the words on these pages never get spoken out loud, they will be here. Maybe for the grandkids. Or maybe for the day when your words don't come out right. You can run to get this book, open to this page, and place it in the hands of someone who needs to know, *This is what God has done for me.*

I'm going to prompt you, but the story you're writing is yours. You write however God leads. One quick thought: A good story includes the kind of details people connect with. Try to be more specific than vague. For instance, in my own life, I could say, *Things didn't turn out like I'd hoped,* or I could be more specific and say, *I was divorced and became a single mom.*

For some of you, life before being redeemed was every day until last week! For others, you can't even remember the first day you believed, so work with these first prompts, depending on your own journey.

*Describe your life before you believed in Jesus, or before you began living what you believe.*

*Before believing, where did your security or happiness come from?*

*How did the life you were living let you down?*

*Can you remember exactly where you were when you understood God's love was personal and for you? Who else was there? What was being said?*

*Did you struggle with the idea of God's love? His forgiveness? What were your struggles? Intellectual? Emotional?*

*Why did you decide to believe in Jesus?*

*Do you know the exact day you believed? Season of life? When?*

*Are there specific changes/differences in your life since you became a follower of Jesus? What are they?*

*Now, look back to Psalm 107. After writing your story, so far, write the
line or words from the psalm that seem even more personal to you now.*

# READ AND MEDITATE

*TODAY'S READING: PSALMS 55–57*

### MY DAY 20 PRAYER FOR YOU

*Father, will You teach this one, Your redeemed, how to say so? Will You help her remember
her story? Give her ease in the remembering and great joy in what You have done. Give her
hope for what can be and all she can become. Lord, bless this storyteller, and thank You for
being her Redeemer, her Savior, her Friend. Because of Your Son, amen and amen.*

How are your 40 days of prayer coming? Stay strong if you are running strong. Jump back
in if you have fallen away. These days are not about rules. These days are about beginning
to practice what we hope to become. Don't give up on trying to pray every day. This is the
power time. Run into the arms of your loving Father.

# RESPOND IN PRAYER

A Bible that's falling apart usually belongs to someone who isn't.[2]
**C.H. SPURGEON**

**DAY 21**

# A REASON TO WORSHIP

Hello, my redeemed friend!

I'm thrilled for us to study what it means to live as the redeemed.

From the moment of our salvation, God's intent with the rest of our lives on earth is that we'd be changed into the image of His Son, Jesus. The better story is lived by the woman who continues being redeemed. The one who keeps trusting God's better plan. His better purpose. His better ways.

I have been changed by this.

> **Worship has been misunderstood as something that arises from a feeling which "comes upon you," but it is vital that we understand that it is rooted in a conscious act of the will, to serve and obey the Lord Jesus Christ.[3]**
> **GRAHAM KENDRICK**

This woman I am today is a better version of me than I have ever been. It's the version of me that looks more like Christ. And yet, there is a road still to travel. There is more to become.

The journey requires I continue toward surrender—I continue toward being redeemed.

## ALL IS WORSHIP

The Redeemer makes us new, redeemed people. Redeemed people worship the Lord for His steadfast love and mercy. I am redeemed and grateful beyond words, and I long to worship my Redeemer. To reflect His glory and His grace.

Worship, however, is one of the areas in my Christian life where I have felt great inadequacy. When I only understood worship as "something you do," I never felt like I was getting it right. Can you relate to that? I wanted to worship God the way the Bible wanted me to worship. One day, the Holy Spirit finally opened my heart to explore this thing called *worship*. If my heart is intended to worship God, then I want it to meet its purpose.

Learning more about worship meant moving beyond my traditions and opening my heart to the Bible's instruction, investigating the many forms of worship in our culture. Worship bands. Choral worship. Meditative worship. Liturgical worship. Responsive readings. Worship dance. Worshipful prayer. Art as worship. Silent retreats. Prayer retreats. Nature walks. Hands up. Hands down. Flags. Banners. Hula as worship. (Not kidding. It's one of the most beautiful things I've ever witnessed.) I know I'm probably missing something, but here's the deal: I found out I love it all. Finally opening my heart in this area gave me such an appreciation for every honest act of heartfelt, biblical worship.

But here's the ridiculous part: While my worship appreciation increased, my personal "acts of worship" still never felt like enough. Not emotional enough. Not pure enough. Not intense enough. Not prayerful enough. Not grateful enough. (Note to all of you: this is where overthinking will get you in trouble.)

*Have you ever struggled with the "doing" of worship? Explain.*

If you've dealt with some of the same feelings, I'm hoping today helps set you free to worship God with your life. The goal of salvation is to produce worshipers—the redeemed are made worshipers at the moment of our salvation. We are worshipers!

## TWO MAIN THOUGHTS

**1. In the Bible, worship is many times spoken of as an act or expression of our praise.** *Proskuneo* means *to bow down, to prostrate oneself, to kiss the hand.* It is honor paid to God and that is why we come together, to give honor to God. An expression of reverence and adoration to God.[4] Worship comes from the overflow of a grateful heart. We worship God personally in our everyday lives, and we come together as the body of Christ as an act of worship. Some would have you believe that worship is a "private matter." We can, and do, worship God privately, but the Bible never leaves worship as a private matter.

*Look up the Bible passages below. Then beside each passage, write down why the people are responding to God with worship.*

*Exodus 4:31*

*Psalm 95:1-3*

*Hebrews 12:28*

*Now, turn over to 1 Chronicles 16:29 and fill in the blanks below:*

*Ascribe to the Lord the _____ due his name; bring an offering and come before him! Worship the Lord in the splendor of _____.*

When you first believe in Jesus, there is a deep and immediate gratefulness for the unearned forgiveness of sin, the assurance of God's love, the promise of heaven, the restoration of our relationship to God, and the sacrifice of Jesus.

The more we grow in the knowledge of Christ, the more we mature as believers. As a result, our gratefulness is ever-increasing.

*When you remember your own salvation, what are you grateful for today? Why?*

*If worship is an expression of gratefulness to God, how do you express your worship to the Lord?*

**2. Worship is how we're meant to live our lives every moment of every day.** Here is where God finally settled my "not enough" worries about worship.

*Read the following passages and underline words concerning how we are to worship.*

But the hour is coming, and is now here, when the true worshipers will worship the Father in spirit and truth, for the Father is seeking such people to worship him. God is spirit, and those who worship him must worship in spirit and truth.
**JOHN 4:23-24**

And whatever you do, in word or deed, do everything in the name of the Lord Jesus, giving thanks to God the Father through him.
**COLOSSIANS 3:17**

> I appeal to you therefore, brothers, by the mercies of God, to present
> your bodies as a living sacrifice, holy and acceptable to God, which
> is your spiritual worship. Do not be conformed to this world, but be
> transformed by the renewal of your mind, that by testing you may discern
> what is the will of God, what is good and acceptable and perfect.
> **ROMANS 12:1-2**

Worship is some days gathering with other believers and singing songs in church. But the definition of *worship* in the Bible goes further. Worship for believers is so much more. The worship God desires means submitting my entire life to be transformed, becoming a reflection of His glory. All of life is intended to be worship for the redeemed. In other words, "Worship is about what you live for."[5]

Those words gave such clarity to me. If worship is about what you live for, then I need to ask, *What am I living for? What is the focus of my attention? The desire of my heart? What drives me? Moves me? Inspires me?*

All of life is worship. We cannot turn off our worship or stop being vessels of worship. Humans were made to worship. In Week 5, we'll talk more about this whole idea, but the evidence of our lives will make it clear. We will either worship the one, true God, or we worship idols—but either way, all of life is worship.

With this understanding of worship, I can truly say I long to worship God with my life. I long to live for God. My acts of worship come from a desire to please God, but on their own, they would never be enough. Yet they are enough because each act, word, thought, feeling, and song I sing is hidden in Christ, my Savior. The Redeemer covers me and makes my worship acceptable and pleasing to God. Just like my life, my acts of worship are being redeemed. And praise the Lord, I don't have to worry about *doing* worship right.

The greater act of obedience is keeping a check on my desire. How will I know if I am worshiping God in spirit and in truth? My life will proclaim the truth by:

> The things I make important
> The objects that hold my attention
> The way I spend my time
> The way I work
> The way I relate to others.

My life, and yours, will shout the truth of our heart's desire.

# READ AND MEDITATE

*TODAY'S READING: PSALMS 58–60*

**MY DAY 21 PRAYER FOR YOU**

*Lord, we long to know all You have revealed to us. All You have done for us. All You have promised to us. Fill our hearts afresh with gratefulness—the kind of gratefulness that leads us to worship. Help us to worship with our voices. Worship with our obedience. Worship with our lives. Be exalted by our desires, Lord. Come give this one a sweet awareness of Your presence. Teach her to worship. In the sweetest name we know, Jesus, amen and amen.*

# RESPOND IN PRAYER

There is nothing more hopeful than the thought that things can be different.[6]
**JOHN ELDRIDGE**

DAY 22

# THE NEW HAS COME

When you belong to God, Satan has lost his hold on you for all eternity (John 10:28). All he has left is to try to render the rest of your life on earth powerless for the kingdom of God. Some of the ways Satan causes believers to live powerlessly include confusing us with unbiblical teaching, distracting us from what we believe, and tempting us to return to our old lives.

*How do you relate to any of those tactics? Explain.*

Here's the thing, too many of us are easy prey because we just don't know Whose we are. We don't yet understand what a really big deal it is to belong to God. Satan's greatest desire is for us to continue to live insecurely, uncertainly, anxiously, and doubtfully about where we before with God. But that kind of life is not what the Bible teaches. God has made clear declarations concerning the redeemed.

**When you are redeemed, your relationship with God has changed. Your life and mission here on earth have changed. Your future life in eternity has changed.**

We're going to take a few days to read and rejoice through these important statements from the Bible. I hope these declarations become lists you look at from time to time. The redeemed need reminders because the new creation is inclined to forget.

## BORN AGAIN

When our South African son, Storm, came to live in our family, he'd been a Christian for about a year. One evening at a restaurant, a television was playing in the background and the person reading the news said, "72 percent of born-again Christians responded" in such-and-such a way. Storm turned to our table and asked, "What is 'born again'?" When we describe ourselves to the world, words like *saved* and *born again* are very biblical, but so very confusing without more of the story.

*What are some other examples of confusing ways we talk about our faith?*

*When I'm with a group of people who may not understand Bible words, I usually tell them I am "a follower of Jesus." What words do you use? Why?*

*Read John 3:1-7. Who comes to Jesus and what was his position?*

*How did he know Jesus was from God?*

*Who can see the kingdom of heaven (v. 3)?*

*According to verse 6, when a person is born on earth (the first birth), she is born of _____. When she believes in Jesus, she is born of the _____ (born again).*

The one who is born again has become a new creation with a new life, new promises, new hope.

## BEHOLD

Let's retrace our steps. Sin separated us from God, but the redeemed are restored to relationship with God. When we believe in Jesus, we are "in Christ." We have a new relationship with God. We are restored to God.

Therefore, if anyone is in Christ, he is a new creation. The old has passed away; behold, the new has come. All this is from God, who through Christ reconciled us to himself and gave us the ministry of reconciliation; that is, in Christ God was reconciling the world to himself, not counting their trespasses against them, and entrusting to us the message of reconciliation. Therefore, we are ambassadors for Christ, God making his appeal through us. We implore you on behalf of Christ, be reconciled to God.
2 CORINTHIANS 5:17-20

*In the passage above, underline the phrase, **the old has passed away.***

Let's take a second to look at exactly what that means for you and me. *Old* means *what has existed since the beginning,* and it's used here as a reference to our old condition.[8] Our old spiritual condition is our old sin nature and death. *Passed away* means *to go, come to an end, disappear*. So let's put these together: Spiritual death has gone. Come to an end. Passed away. At the moment of salvation, that old condition is removed from you forever. You will never be spiritually dead again! Somebody holler, *Hallelujah!* Even before we talk about all that becomes new, this is such great news.

*Now, go back to the passage and draw a box around the word **behold.***

Whenever we read "behold," the writer wants us to stop and pay attention. Something amazing is happening! I love this explanation:

**The word *behold* is intended to convey a delighted sense of surprise and pleasure: *"Look at this—isn't it amazing! Here is a person who has altered for the better right across the board!"* It is alarming, then, to observe that some who claim to be Christians seem virtually the same as they always were.[9]**

*Fill in these blanks with the words directly after "behold." This is what we're supposed to stop and pay attention to:*

*The _____ has _____.*

*Now, go back through the passage and circle all the phrases that describe our new, redeemed relationship with God.*

**In Christ** can mean several things that are not mutually exclusive: that one belongs to Christ, that one lives in the sphere of Christ's power, that one is united with Christ, or that one is part of the body of Christ, the believing community. Paul's assumption is that being in Christ should bring about a radical change in a person's life.[7]

## When God Makes All Things New

1. *We will be holy, having the glory of God.* We can make progress here on earth as we allow the Holy Spirit to guide us, but our hearts long for the day we will finally be delivered from the temptation of evil and sin (Rev. 21:9-11).

2. *We will have a new body* (Phil. 3:20-21; 2 Cor. 5:1-5).

3. *Creation will be new and glorious* (Rom. 8:19-22).

4. *We will see God.* God is with us now, but He has called us to live by faith. One day, our faith becomes sight, and we will behold Him as He is (Rev. 22:4).

*New* means *recently made*, but it's even more than that. The implication is that the new creation (me and you) is better than the old women we used to be.[10] Here's something I want you to notice: This passage does not say, "all things" are made new. That's our future promise in Revelation 21:

And he who was seated on the throne said, "Behold, I am making all things new." Also he said, "Write this down, for these words are trustworthy and true."
**REVELATION 21:5**

All things do not become new for the believer at our salvation. Our spiritual condition is immediately new, but becoming a "new person" happens through years of spiritual growth. The new that comes immediately at salvation is:

• A new spiritual nature—Christ in us, our new nature
• A new spiritual destination—eternity in heaven
• A new spiritual power—the indwelling of the Holy Spirit
• A new spiritual potential—to be like Christ.

Because of the indwelling of the Holy Spirit, we have a new potential that we could not have before salvation. Just like our free choice to choose salvation, we also have the free choice to allow the Holy Spirit to guide us.

One of the greatest frustrations for every believer is that our new spiritual condition comes to live alongside our old earthly body. Paul talks about the battle between our flesh and our spirits. Do you remember when we talked about this on our first day of the study? It's the battle that makes us want to cry to God, "I can't."

Is this all beginning to make a little more sense to you? Do you understand why you can't just say to someone, "Hey girl, you're saved. All things are new! Buck up. Let's get on with it. Just stop acting like that. Just stop being addicted to that. You're a follower of Jesus. What's wrong with you?"

Maybe you've actually said some of those words to yourself. Beat yourself up. *I'm a new creation. What's wrong with me?* Take heart, my friend, we're in this thing together. Becoming a new creation is the rest of the story for the redeemed. But for today, let's just rest right here and behold: The old has passed away. The new has come. And the gift of God's grace will never be undone.

# READ AND MEDITATE

*TODAY'S READING: PSALMS 61–63*

**MY DAY 22 PRAYER FOR YOU**

*Lord, over this dear one, I pray the angels declare, "Behold! The old woman has passed away, the new has come." Father, let her come fully alive as Your new creation. Give her eyes to behold the grace of her new spirit, her new nature, her new potential. Let the goodness of Your gift lift her soul today. Stop her self-shaming thoughts and her self-defeating attitudes. Teach her how to behold. In the name of Jesus, amen.*

Out of 100 men, one will read the Bible, the other 99 will read the Christian.[11]
**DWIGHT L. MOODY**

# RESPOND IN PRAYER

Very few . . . behave as if God is a God of love, forgiveness, gentleness and compassion. They see God as someone to cower before . . . Do we wake up every morning amazed that we are loved by God? Do we allow our day to be shaped by God's desire to relate to us?[12]
**PHILIP YANCEY**

DAY 23

# A NEW CREATION

As I've told you several times, this study is about knowing who you are in Christ and what He has done for you, but the purpose of this study is so much greater.

My prayer is that you will be redeemed—and then live redeemed. I'm praying for redeemed marriages and redeemed kids. Redeemed attitudes. Redeemed spending. Redeemed talk. Redeemed careers. Redeemed friendships. Redeemed churches. Redeemed laughter. Redeemed healing. Redeemed habits. Redeemed addictions. I'm all in, begging God to radically, by the power of heaven, come into your house and your office and your classroom and your car and your backyard—to right where you are this minute. I'm asking Him, for His glory and His kingdom, to redeem His people.

The 40 days of prayer in this study are so intentional. If anything in our lives is going to be redeemed, the power of God is required. The most spiritually powerful tool we have is the power of intimate prayer. I hope you'll stay with it.

This next quote by Spurgeon is pretty intense, but it gets to the heart of my passion, so I wanted to share it with you.

**If sinners be damned, at least let them leap to Hell over our bodies. And if they will perish, let them perish with our arms about their knees. . . . Let no one go there unwarned and unprayed for.**[13]
**C.H. SPURGEON**

Most of you are not leaping into hell! But too many of us are fast asleep and snoring on the way to heaven. If it feels like I'm trying to grab you at the knees and you're dragging this pestering Bible teacher along with you, it's because I'll do almost anything for you to understand the powerful, lavish gift you've been given. Christ alone has the power to radically change everything in your every day, in your this-afternoon life. I cannot do it for you, but praise God, Jesus can.

At the moment we believe, we are permanently and eternally set apart for God. That can never change. It's our new position as a new creation. And you need to know what that means!

## YOUR NEW LIFE WITH GOD

As we work through these next statements, I'll ask you to read or respond here and there. I'll also make a few comments along the way. But here's the main thing I want you to do after each declaration: I want you to rewrite the statement beginning with words like *I am* or *I have*. I want you to make these truths as personal as you can. *All* of these belong to you. Learning to live every day in the truth is hard enough, but goodness gracious, let's at least know what the Bible says we are!

**1. YOUR SINS ARE FORGIVEN. I** _____.

> In him we have redemption through his blood, the forgiveness
> of our trespasses, according to the riches of his grace.
> **EPHESIANS 1:7**

Too many of us don't live like it's true. We are forgiven people. Undeserved and unworthy, yet, by God's grace, we are forgiven.

> *When you meet a woman who knows she's forgiven, what is the most*
> *noticeable thing about her? How does someone live like she's forgiven?*
> *(I'll give you a few ideas, but I want you to add more):*

> *She learns to make eye contact again.*
> *There is no more shame to hang her head over.*
> *Giving what she has been given, by forgiving someone who doesn't deserve it.*

**2. YOU ARE MADE RIGHTEOUS IN THE EYES OF GOD. I** _____.

> For our sake he made him to be sin who knew no sin, so that
> in him we might become the righteousness of God.
> **2 CORINTHIANS 5:21**

I always think of righteousness as being in "right standing with God." No one is ever able to attain righteousness on their own. The Pharisees thought of themselves as righteous and imitated a false righteousness, but they could not make themselves righteous. Neither can we. In Christ, we have been brought into the inner circle. Moved up to the head table. Seated in the roped-off seats. We have become His masterpiece (Eph. 2:10), trophies of His grace (Eph. 2:4-7).

To be in right standing with God is the greatest acceptance we could aspire to. And yet, full acceptance (righteousness) is already ours in Jesus. No striving required. What if we could see our attempts at "being accepted" in this world for what they really are— a striving for lesser things. We are fully accepted by God. Why are we begging someone or something to give us what we already have? We have been set free!

Have you been striving for acceptance? Are you tired? Disappointed? I'm so blessed to tell you that you can lay it down. The redeemed are accepted by God. All the other striving is like chasing the wind.

*What will you lay down today?*


**3. YOU ARE ADOPTED INTO THE FAMILY OF GOD, GIVEN AN INHERITANCE FROM GOD. I _____**

_____.

You belong to God. God is your Father. We are the adopted sons and daughters. We belong to the family of God.

> But to all who did receive him, who believed in his name,
> he gave the right to become children of God.
> JOHN 1:12

> But when the fullness of time had come, God sent forth his Son, born of woman, born under the law, to redeem those who were under the law, so that we might receive adoption as sons. And because you are sons, God has sent the Spirit of his Son into our hearts, crying, "Abba! Father!" So you are no longer a slave, but a son, and if a son, then an heir through God.
> GALATIANS 4:4-7

> . . . giving thanks to the Father, who has qualified you to share in the inheritance of the saints in light.
> COLOSSIANS 1:12

What kinds of things does a daughter do? Asks her Father for advice. Learns to get along in the family with her brothers and sisters.

*What else does a daughter do? List a few ideas.*

**4. YOU HAVE ACCESS TO GOD. I** _____.

> Therefore, since we have been justified by faith, we have peace with God through our Lord Jesus Christ. Through him we have also obtained access by faith into this grace in which we stand, and we rejoice in hope of the glory of God.
> **ROMANS 5:1-2**

> Since then we have a great high priest who has passed through the heavens, Jesus, the Son of God, let us hold fast our confession. For we do not have a high priest who is unable to sympathize with our weaknesses, but one who in every respect has been tempted as we are, yet without sin. Let us then with confidence draw near to the throne of grace, that we may receive mercy and find grace to help in time of need.
> **HEBREWS 4:14-16**

Jesus became our High Priest so that we may have direct access to God. We are no longer far off and separated from God. We have direct access to Him in prayer. In confession. In thanksgiving. In praise.

*When do you have access to God?*

**5. YOU ARE A CITIZEN OF HEAVEN. I** _____.

> But our citizenship is in heaven, and from it we await a Savior, the Lord Jesus Christ, who will transform our lowly body to be like his glorious body, by the power that enables him even to subject all things to himself.
> **PHILIPPIANS 3:20-21**

The residency of the redeemed has changed. You are a citizen of heaven. You will spend eternity with God. Construction on your heavenly home has begun (John 3:16; 14:1-4). But you and I are not yet home. Feeling homesick is not uncommon for the redeemed. The soul longs to live where it was made to be.

*Do you ever feel like this world is not your home? Like you're not there yet? When have you felt that way recently? Journal a few thoughts.*

**6. YOU HAVE PEACE WITH GOD. I** _____.

> But now in Christ Jesus you who once were far off have been brought near by the blood of Christ. For he himself is our peace, who has made us both one and has broken down in his flesh the dividing wall of hostility by abolishing the law of commandments expressed in ordinances, that he might create in himself one new man in place of the two, so making peace, and might reconcile us both to God in one body through the cross, thereby killing the hostility. And he came and preached peace to you who were far off and peace to those who were near.
> **EPHESIANS 2:13-17**

I guess every person I know is looking for peace, one way or another. What if the redeemed stopped looking for this world to give us what only God can give? What if we really and truly lived in the peace that comes from knowing Whose we are? When God's peace becomes your real peace, the Bible calls it "the peace . . . which surpasses all understanding" (Phil. 4:7). Wouldn't every day be better if we learned to live in His peace and not our own?

*What are the top three areas of your life where it's time to declare God's peace (not chaos) belongs to you?*

# READ AND MEDITATE
*TODAY'S READING: PSALMS 64–66*

### MY DAY 23 PRAYER FOR YOU

*Father, make this new creation more than she's ever been. Make her more than different; she needs to become better than before. May Your declarations become to her peace, power, and strength. In Jesus' name, amen.*

# RESPOND IN PRAYER
We see who we were. God sees who we're becoming.[14]
**BOB GOFF**

_____
_____
_____

DAY 24

# A FAR BETTER STORY

I loved the study yesterday! Sometimes studying the Bible is like striking oil in your own backyard. It's been yours all this time; it came with the deed to the house, but you just didn't know it was there. Let's keep rolling—it's getting fun now!

Let's do "You Are's" today. As one who has been redeemed by God's love:

You are a child of God (John 1:12).
You are promised an abundant life (John 10:10).
You are a branch of Jesus Christ (John 15:5).
You are a friend of God (John 15:15).
You are chosen to bear the fruit of God (John 15:16).
You are saved from the wrath of God's judgment (Rom. 5:9).
You are no longer a slave to sin (Rom. 6:18).
You are not condemned (Rom. 8:1-2).
You are promised a new body (Rom. 8:23).
You are being helped in your weakness (Rom. 8:26-27).
You are no longer separated from the love of God (Rom. 8:31-39).
You are God's temple (1 Cor. 6:19-20).
You are Christ's ambassador (2 Cor. 5:20).
You are not under the curse of the law (Gal. 3:13).
You are free (Gal. 5:1).
You are sealed by the Holy Spirit (Eph. 1:13).
You are made for good works (Eph. 2:10).
You are confident God will complete the work He began in you (Phil. 1:6).
You are able to do all things through Christ who strengthens you (Phil. 4:13).
You are delivered from the domain of Satan (Col. 1:13).
You are complete in Christ (Col. 2:9-10).
You are hidden with Christ (Col. 3:1-4).
You are filled with a spirit of power, love, and self-control (2 Tim. 1:7).
You are promised life instead of death (1 Pet. 3:18).
You are supported by your Advocate, Jesus Christ (1 John 2:1).

*Today, we're doing things a little differently. Instead of guiding you step by step, I want you to stop for a few minutes and pray. As you pray, will you look back over the "You Are's" list and ask the Lord to direct your study? Then choose where you will spend your time today. Find those passages. Read God's promises. Decide where God is asking you to live that truth in your life. I'm leaving you room to work below.*

*God's promise:*

*The passage:*

*My assignment:*

*God's promise:*

*The passage:*

*My assignment:*

*God's promise:*

*The passage:*

*My assignment:*

*God's promise:*

*The passage:*

*My assignment:*

*There is a far better story to be lived than the one most of us have known. Do you sense that's true for you? Your family? Your mission in this world? Explain.*

The next two weeks of this study are about living redeemed lives. May God give us a deep, passionate yearning. May He fill us with grace upon grace as we make this journey together. I pray something in your spirit is thinking, *Let's do this. I'm ready to run.*

# READ AND MEDITATE

*TODAY'S READING: PSALMS 67–70*

**MY DAY 24 PRAYER FOR YOU**

*Father, will You surprise this one with a new confidence in Your Word? She can seek You. She can learn from You. She can apply Your truth to her life. Lord, bless her and multiply her joy in Your presence, amen and amen.*

# RESPOND IN PRAYER

Never be afraid to trust an unknown future to a known God.[15]
**CORRIE TEN BOOM**

**DAY 25**

# READ, MEDITATE, & PRAY

Remember . . .

> Fear not, you worm Jacob, you men of Israel!
> I am the one who helps you, declares the LORD;
> your Redeemer is the Holy One of Israel.
> **ISAIAH 41:14**

## READ AND MEDITATE

*TODAY'S READING: PSALMS 71–75*

**MY DAY 25 PRAYER FOR YOU**

*Sweet Jesus, be close to this one. Do not let her wander away. Take away every lonesome thought. Every hopeless declaration. Restore her. Renew her. Set her free. Because of Your Son, amen.*

## RESPOND IN PRAYER

Faith is deliberate confidence in the character of God whose ways you may not understand at the time.[16]
**OSWALD CHAMBERS**

_____

_____

_____

_____

_____

_____

_____

_____

_____

DAY 26

# READ, MEDITATE, & PRAY

The goal of being redeemed is to become like Jesus. To bear His image. To display His countenance. To bestow His grace.

No chapter in your story is unredeemable.

## READ AND MEDITATE

TODAY'S READING: PSALMS 76–80

**MY DAY 26 PRAYER FOR YOU**

*Father, will You do what this one could never imagine? Redeem what seems lost. Restore what has been broken. Revive what had been buried. Make her new, Lord. Inside and out, in secret and in plain view, make her new. By Your power and for Your glory, amen.*

## RESPOND IN PRAYER

We want to avoid suffering, death, sin, ashes. But we live in a world crushed and broken and torn, a world God Himself visited to redeem. We receive his poured-out life, and being allowed the high privilege of suffering with Him, may then pour ourselves out for others.[17]
**ELISABETH ELLIOT**

# SESSION 5: VIEWER GUIDE

**REDEEMED FOR FREEDOM**

For whosoever shall call upon the name of the Lord shall be saved.
**ROMANS 10:13 (KJV)**

For he will command his angels concerning you
to guard you in all your ways.
**PSALM 91:11**

The moment we are _____, the chains are _____.

In the same way we also, when we were children, were enslaved to the elementary principles of the world. But when the fullness of time had come, God sent forth his Son, born of woman, born under the law, to redeem those who were under the law, so that we might receive adoption as sons. And because you are sons, God has sent the Spirit of his Son into our hearts, crying, "Abba! Father!" So you are no longer a slave, but a son, and if a son, then an heir through God.
**GALATIANS 4:3-7**

When we are redeemed, we are _____ into the family of God.

When we are adopted, we are treated as a _____.

When we are redeemed, being a _____ to sin
is _____.

Video sessions available for purchase
at *www.lifeway.com/redeemed*

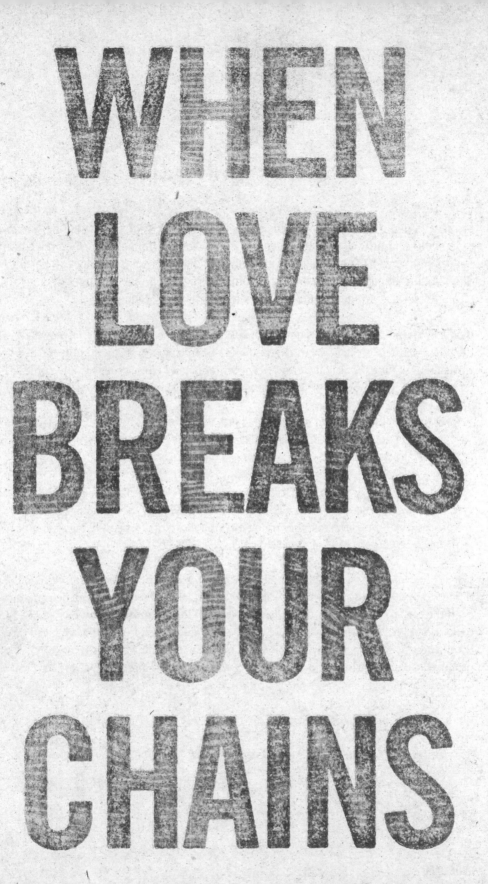

DAY 27

# SO YOU'LL BE FREE

My heart's desire and prayer for this study is that, first, your soul would be redeemed, and next, your actual, everyday life would be redeemed. When a woman begins to live what she believes, there will be visual, external evidence in her life! She is being changed heart, soul, and mind. Her relationships change. Choices change. Motives change. The Bible calls that kind of evidence fruit.

By the grace of God, our chains have been broken. And also by His grace, we now have the power of the Holy Spirit to throw off those broken chains and run into the freedom Christ bought for us. This journey between salvation and being home with the Lord in heaven is about learning to live in freedom.

> For freedom Christ has set us free; stand firm therefore,
> and do not submit again to a yoke of slavery.
> **GALATIANS 5:1**

We've been set free so we can live free! Its time to throw off the chains, take off those prison clothes, and leave that jail cell behind. We are free! But learning to live in freedom is a process the Bible refers to as becoming mature followers of Christ, being sanctified, growing up in Christ, or being transformed.

Just as much as Christ accomplished our redemption from sin, He also accomplished the fullness of our sanctification. That means we can be changed! We have been delivered from the certainty of death to the certainty of eternal life, but until then, there is still a life to live on earth. And while we are here, God's main ambition for us is to be changed into the likeness of His Son. We are promised eternal life with God in heaven, but we are also promised a life in Christ here on earth. Being changed here is preparing us for eternity with God in heaven.

But how does God want us to change?

*Turn in your Bible to 2 Corinthians 5:15 and fill in the blanks below.*

*He died for all, that those who live might no longer _____ _____ _____ but for _____ who for their sake _____ and was _____.*

God wants the people who live for themselves to become people who live for Him. Whether you've been a Christian for two days or fifty years, at any given moment, we are all either moving toward God or away from Him. Either living for ourselves or living for Him. Focused on becoming more like Him or focused on ourselves. Being redeemed in our character is a process. We have to learn how to live for God. We have to learn not to live for ourselves. Our everyday lives will become the evidence that we are growing.

But here's the problem. Becoming like Christ doesn't come naturally to us. It is a work of the Holy Spirit. When we learn how to respond to the Holy Spirit, we learn how to connect God's grace to our struggles—and that has the power to redeem everything.

*Take a look at 2 Peter 1:3-9 and answer the questions that follow.*

[3] His divine power has granted to us all things that pertain to life and godliness, through the knowledge of him who called us to his own glory and excellence, [4] by which he has granted to us his precious and very great promises, so that through them you may become partakers of the divine nature, having escaped from the corruption that is in the world because of sinful desire. [5] For this very reason, make every effort to supplement your faith with virtue, and virtue with knowledge, [6] and knowledge with self-control, and self-control with steadfastness, and steadfastness with godliness, [7] and godliness with brotherly affection, and brotherly affection with love. [8] For if these qualities are yours and are increasing, they keep you from being ineffective or unfruitful in the knowledge of our Lord Jesus Christ. [9] For whoever lacks these qualities is so nearsighted that he is blind, having forgotten that he was cleansed from his former sins.
**2 PETER 1:3-9**

*Verses 3-4 describe our salvation. In verse 3, what does the divine power of God give to believers?*

*And what two things does God call each one of us to?*

_____ *and* _____

*To be partakers of the divine nature means we are "in Christ." In verse 4, what have we been granted from God?*

*And what have we escaped?*

*Verses 5-8 describe the process of sanctification, growing up as mature followers of Jesus. Look at verse 8. What are two benefits of increasing (becoming more like Jesus)?*

*Now look at verse 9. The passage gives us two reasons believers do not change. What are they?*

*1.*

*2.*

As believers and followers of Jesus, we do not live effective and fruitful lives when we become nearsighted to the point of blindness or when we forget what God has done. We forget who we are in Christ. We forget this journey is about being changed into His image. And we forget we are still sinners, who every single day need the Savior.

The day we believe in Jesus, we join the family of God, but we have not yet arrived. We don't just coast on into heaven. The day we believe is the day spiritual growth begins. Until He calls us home to be with Him, God's unwavering commitment is making us like Christ.

*When you think about your own spiritual growth, have there been times you grew more than others? Times you went backward instead of forward?*

*Choose any that apply below:*

*_____ I'm too old to change.*

*_____ I don't really see other people changing, so why should I?*

*_____ I'm so young and fun, there's nothing I really want to change!*

_____ *Change is hard, and I'm too tired to think about it.*

_____ *I've tried to change a few things, but I can't.*

_____ *I'm desperate to change.*

Have you ever watched the show on HGTV called *Fixer Upper?* In Waco, Texas, Chip and Joanna Gaines help families choose an old, run-down house to completely renovate. There is usually some dilapidated house most people would drive right past or just tear down. And almost every show, the couple viewing the property says something like, "I just can't see how this can work. I can't envision anything better. I certainly can't envision anything wonderful." Then an hour goes by and by the end of the show, the couple stands outside their new home, anxiously waiting for the reveal. You know how this goes. Walls are pulled back. Eyes are opened. And what they see is beyond anything they could have ever imagined.

Well, my beautiful friend, this is your *Fixer Upper* life. Maybe everything in your life is a mess and all the people who drive by can see it falling apart. Maybe things look okay on the outside, but the unseen structure is rotten and crumbling. Maybe you've tried to do a few renovations on your own, but you ran out of steam or the problems were beyond your ability to repair. Here's what I want you to know: God sees your life in ways you cannot. He sees what you can become. Not only does He have the power, but He is also creative beyond your wildest imagination. And let me tell you something: When your life is changed by the power of God into something better than anyone could imagine, He gets all the glory. He gets all the praise. Your life becomes a testimony and a witness to His goodness and grace. People will see what He's done and go to Him with their own lives, saying, *Lord, what You did for her, do for me!*

> *Turn to Philippians 1:6, where Paul is writing to people growing in their faith. Below, rewrite verse 6 as the promise God has made to you personally.*

My question for us is if God is faithful to complete what He begins in us, will we be faithful to grow in Him? Will you coast to heaven with all the consequences it brings, or will you commit to grow in your faith?

Because God is able and because He keeps His promises, we have hope.

He is our Redeemer.
We can be redeemed.
Our lives can be changed.
We can live a better story.

# READ AND MEDITATE

*TODAY'S READING: PSALMS 81–85*

**MY DAY 27 PRAYER FOR YOU**

*Father, speak Your truth so sweetly to this one. Tell her Your promises again. Tell her there is more waiting than she can imagine. Remind her there is a process. There is a journey. There is hope. In Jesus' name, amen.*

# RESPOND IN PRAYER

Humiliation is the beginning of sanctification.[1]
**JOHN DONNE**

_____
_____
_____
_____
_____
_____
_____
_____
_____
_____
_____
_____
_____
_____
_____
_____
_____
_____

DAY 28

# SO YOU CAN SEE

I'm just gonna go ahead and tell you, today might be a little hard for some of us to swallow. And here's the reason: Most of us just don't think we're all that bad.

I know this because I know myself. If I'm not careful, my natural inclination is to minimize my own sinfulness. Make excuses in my head. Present reasonable explanations out loud. God's grace has freed me from the penalty of my sin, but I still have a sin disease. I am still living in a fallen body with a fallen mind. I am not home yet.

This world is a tough place to be many days. Not only has the whole world been broken since the fall, but Satan is also alive and well. In the New Testament, the apostle Paul didn't gloss over life's difficulties, writing many times of the afflictions, persecution, burdens, and pressures he faced. In 2 Corinthians, he wrote,

> For we do not want you to be unaware, brothers, of the affliction we experienced in Asia. For we were so utterly burdened beyond our strength that we despaired of life itself. Indeed, we felt that we had received the sentence of death.
> **2 CORINTHIANS 1:8-9a**

But even in the great affliction of this fallen world, we are called to respond and react as followers of Jesus. Paul continued,

> But that was to make us rely not on ourselves but on God who raises the dead.
> **2 CORINTHIANS 1:9b**

In case you haven't noticed, there may be difficulty and there may be blessing, but there will always be something. Life just keeps coming! We will either respond to life from our old sin nature or learn to rely on God. To grow in Christlikeness means we must see ourselves as we truly are. We still drag broken chains that need to fall. We still battle sin. We're still prone to wander.

God says His grace will both enable us and deliver us. His grace will produce wisdom, character, and strength in us. He promises His grace will be sufficient in every circumstance and struggle we face. I can't control what comes to me, but how I respond comes from inside me. That is the place God wants to change.

Take a look at the following list and circle the places where you currently struggle the most.

| | | |
|---|---|---|
| Parenting | Ministry | Envy |
| Work | Church | Authority |
| Health | Scheduling | Anger |
| Marriage | Culture | Resentment |
| Finances | Extended Family | Blame |
| Friendships | School | Disappointment |
| Relationships | Children | Temptation |

As you think through the current struggles you face, respond to the questions below.

Where do you question God's goodness?


What makes you want to give up on God?


What are you wishing for? If only _____.


When do you slack off studying the Bible and spending time in prayer?


Where are you embarrassed by the way you act/think?


When are you the most unkind?


Where are you blaming God?


When you think of how God sees your life, what do you think He wants you to change?

It's very humbling to stop and look at my life as it is—to realize I'm worse than I knew. To recognize again, I am not able to do this on my own. In order to resist sin, I must stay dependent on God.

The most central and scary step toward being changed is taking responsibility for the way I respond to life. For the sin I invoke.

The way I speak to my children
The way I focus on my own needs
The way I zero in on other people's faults
The way I just do the things I feel like doing.

As painful as it is, we have to see our responses for what they are. We are either choosing from our sin nature, or we are being redeemed and living according to Scripture. Every reaction we have to life flows from the heart. Whatever's going on in your heart will determine how you respond to your problems and your struggles.

Have you ever had a safe friend say something like, "I hear what you're saying, and I totally understand why you'd feel that way, but it seems like there's more. Can you tell me what's really going on in your heart?" It's the same with our sin. It's the same with all of our problems. There is always something deeper going on.

## Our sin problem comes from our heart problem.

Our hearts have not changed because we do not think correctly or we do not believe.

We are still operating in our humanity; left unchecked, we still sin. We shade the truth if we think it'll help. We're selfish and self-protective and self-loathing. We manipulate people and situations. We're quick to say ugly things and jump to conclusions. We lust and envy and boast. We spout judgment. We talk about people behind their backs and give them the silent treatment to their faces. We return evil for evil.

All the days of our journey home, God is calling us to do the ongoing work to recognize our sin, then respond in the deeper places to change. This is powerful inside-out work.

*Turn in your Bibles to Philippians 2. Paul was writing to the church at Philippi. In verses 5-11, Paul recounted the beautiful truth and theology of Christ's sacrifice for us.*

*Look at verse 12. What's the first word of the verse?*

A reminder: Every single time we read the word *therefore* in the Bible, we have to go back and find out what it's there for. *Therefore* points backward to connect what just happened to what is coming. In this case, Paul was going back to the theology of Christ's death to bring it home for our everyday lives. *Therefore* points to the results that should happen in our lives.

*From verses 12-13, fill in the blanks below.*

_____, *my beloved, as you have always obeyed,*
*so now, not only as in my presence but much more in my absence,*
_____ _____ *your own* _____
*with fear and trembling, for it is God who works in you, both to will and to*
*work for his good pleasure.*

Because of what Christ did for us, we are called to become the real life, everyday demonstration of our salvation. We work out our salvation so that we become the out-working of God's redeeming love.

Evidently the church at Philippi had been living in obedience because Paul praised them when he wrote "as you have always obeyed" (v. 12). But look at what he asks them to do with their obedience in his absence: much more. He wants them to turn it up.

In verse 13, Paul was clear about our own inability to work it out. Both the power and the desire to work come from God. Redemption living isn't by our own power or desires.

**God works in you. The verb *works in* means "to put one's capabilities into operation, work, be at work, be active, operate, and be effective." All the capabilities of God are in operation, active, and effective in the work of believers.[2]**

So what does all this mean for you and me? It means that God will give us both the power to change and the desire to be changed.

It also means we are called to do the personal work. The Holy Spirit lives inside of you. He will guide you. Lead you. Help you. And some days, it can almost feel like He's screaming at you! But He does not push some magical button to make you do anything. You and I must do the work of cooperating with the Holy Spirit.

*Why does Paul call this kind of obedience work?*

Because there's no way around it. Learning to live like the redeemed is many days frustrating and exhausting. It can feel like real work. And it can make you tired like work. We may want to skip over it because it's too much like work, but we can't.

Obedience also feels like work because a war is being fought for your heart. The war is raging, and you are living every day smack dab in the middle of a war zone. We want a peacetime life, but the world has gone to war against us.

To keep being changed means we have to do this deeper work. Are you willing to do the work of being redeemed?

Before I let you go, one last thing. Do not let the recognition of your sin become another unhealthy reason to self-condemn. We recognize our sin in order to be made right, not to fall into more sin. If we give our entire selves over to the truths of Scripture, recognizing our sin becomes a reason to celebrate the grace of God. A way to understand the old patterns and habits we fall into. A path to restore relationships here on earth. An opportunity to grow in our faith.

We can be thankful God is not content to leave us the way we are. We can rejoice in the gift of Jesus and our forgiveness.

# READ AND MEDITATE

*TODAY'S READING: PSALMS 86–90*

**MY DAY 28 PRAYER FOR YOU**

You will say that these are very small sins; and doubtless, like all young tempters, you are anxious to be able to report spectacular wickedness. But do remember, the only thing that matters is the extent to which you separate the man from the Enemy. It does not matter how small the sins are provided that their cumulative effect is to edge the man away from the Light and out into the Nothing. Murder is no better than cards if cards can do the trick. Indeed the safest road to Hell is the gradual one— the gentle slope, soft underfoot, without sudden turnings, without milestones, without signposts.

Your affectionate uncle
Screwtape [3]
C.S. LEWIS

*Lord, give this precious heart spiritual eyes to see her sin and a spiritual mind to respond in healthy ways. Give her the desire to work out the salvation she's been given. Keep her far from condemnation, always rejoicing in the grace and mercy of Your love. In Jesus' name, amen.*

# RESPOND IN PRAYER

God has made provision for our holiness. Through Christ He has delivered us from sin's reign so that we now can resist sin. But the responsibility for resisting is ours. God does not do that for us. To confuse the *potential* for resisting (which God provided) with the *responsibility* for resisting (which is ours) is to court disaster in our pursuit of holiness.[4]
**JERRY BRIDGES**

DAY 29

# SO THERE IS ORDER

Yesterday I mentioned having a friend who listens to your problems and then cares enough to ask, "Is something else going on? Something deeper than what you just told me?" I want this study to be like a trusted friend. We could just skim across the top of life and talk about how a Christian can have a better marriage or become a better friend or parent, but the truth is, new relationship strategies will never get to the heart of our problems. Keeping a list of rules won't get us there either. They will not change us; we'll have to go deeper.

By grace, we are saved when we give our hearts to Jesus. And by that same grace, the Holy Spirit who lives in us transforms our hearts until our lives bear the sweet fruit of redemption.

> Redeemed hearts become redeemed relationships.
> Redeemed minds become redeemed homes, churches, neighborhoods, and schools.
> Redeemed vision becomes redeemed purpose, mission, and calling.

We want *things* to change. God wants *people* to change. People are changed when their hearts are transformed by His grace.

## A REORDERED HEART

Yesterday we said our sin problem comes from our heart problem. According to Augustine (A.D. 354-430), our heart problem is our "disordered loves." He believed there was an order to love and wrote that right living requires "an objective and impartial evaluation of things: to love things, that is to say, in the right order, so that you do not love what is not to be loved, or fail to love what is to be loved, or have a greater love for what should be loved less, or an equal love for things that should be loved less or more, or a lesser or greater love for things that should be loved equally."[5]

We struggle with sin because we have disordered hearts. We have made the lesser things the main things. We have put something we love before the God we should love supremely. Our priorities are out of whack.

*Do you see any evidence of "disordered loves" in your own life? Explain.*

When our loves are out of order, the Bible calls it idolatry. Whatever we love more than God becomes the focus of our worship, and therefore, it has become an idol. Here's how Tim Keller defines *idolatry*. An *idol* is:

- **Anything more important to you than God.**

- **Anything that absorbs your heart and imagination more than God.**

- **Anything you seek to give you what only God can give.**

- **Whatever you look at and say, in your heart of hearts, "If I have that, then I'll feel my life has meaning, then I'll know I have value, then I'll feel significant and secure."**

- **Anything [that] becomes more fundamental than God to your happiness, meaning in life, and identity.**[6]

> *When you look at Keller's definitions of "idolatry," how are you convicted in your own heart?*

We all have idols of some sort, and Keller goes on to divide our idols into two categories: deeper idols and surface idols.

**Deeper Idols** are a desire for influence and power; a craving for appreciation, approval, or acceptance; a desire for emotional and physical comfort; or a desire for security and control.

Keller says one of the above is usually more prevalent and becomes our deeper idol. The deeper idol controls our actions and desires and is often well hidden by those enslaved to them.

**Surface Idols** are things like a house, money, sex, possessions, our spouse, our children, or other addictions like drugs, exercise, food, shopping, video games, gambling, pornography, theft, cutting, weight loss, and on and on.

Sometimes, getting rid of the surface idol won't deal with the deeper idol because the purpose of surface idols is to appease and satisfy our deeper idols. For example: a surface idol might be shopping, while the deeper idol is comfort or acceptance.[7]

Sometimes you sign up for a Bible study to learn some things about God, to know your way around the Bible a little better. If that's what you were thinking, you might be a little peeved at me about now. Maybe you didn't have any intention of looking into your own heart or your own life. All I can tell you is that the Word of God will not let us only observe its truths.

*Turn in your Bibles to Hebrews 4:12-13 and respond to the following.*

*The Word of God is _____ and active.*

*The Word is sharper than what?*

*The Word of God pierces and divides what?*

*The Word of God discerns what?*

*Who can hide from the Word of God?*

> **Man's nature . . . is a perpetual factory of idols . . . Man tries to express in his work the sort of God he has inwardly conceived. Therefore the mind begets an idol; the hand gives it birth.**[8]
> **JOHN CALVIN**

To study the Word of God is to be convicted and changed by its truth. Being redeemed means we will be changed at the deepest level of our hearts. The truth of God's Word will guide us. The grace of God's love will keep us. Let's press on.

I know you remember the Ten Commandments. Let's take a look at the first three:

> And God spoke all these words, saying, "I am the LORD your God, who brought you out of the land of Egypt, out of the house of slavery. "You shall have no other gods before me. "You shall not make for yourself a carved image, or any likeness of anything that is in heaven above, or that is in the earth beneath, or that is in the water under the earth. You shall not bow down to them or serve them, for I the LORD your God am a jealous God, visiting the iniquity of the fathers on the children to the third and the fourth generation of those who hate me, but showing steadfast love to thousands of those who love me and keep my commandments. "You shall not take the name of the LORD your God in vain, for the LORD will not hold him guiltless who takes his name in vain."
> **EXODUS 20:1-7**

God was intentional concerning the order of the commandments, so the order is important. The first three commandments focus on the order of our loves. God commands nothing can come before Him in our lives. We are to love Him above everything. When our loves becomes disordered, we worship whatever we love more than God. Jesus affirmed this order when He summed up the greatest commandment like this:

> "Teacher, which is the great commandment in the Law?" And he said to him, "You shall love the Lord your God with all your heart and with all your soul and with all your mind."
> MATTHEW 22:36-37

If anything besides God becomes the greatest love of our hearts, it has also become our idol. John Calvin called the human heart an idol factory because humans are so quick to manufacture a multitude of replacements for God.[9]

How quickly we make good things the supreme thing. We so often worship the created instead of the Creator.

*Turn to Ezekiel 14:3. According to this verse, where do we take our idols?*

God is committed to reclaiming our hearts and remaking us into the image of Christ. There is a war going on for the hearts of believers, and God will fight for our affections. He wants the whole heart—all of us, without distraction, sin, or idols.

Growing in spiritual maturity means removing anything that has become an idol and reaffirming our desire to love God first.

The problem is that most of us aren't very good at being self-aware. We'd rather not look. Taking an honest look at deeper struggles is tough for everybody, but we're going to give it a shot. Being redeemed is too important not to do the very thing that can help us the most.

The past two days, I've been trying to walk us down a little deeper into our hearts, then on a little deeper, and tomorrow, we'll take one more step. But I want to remind you of something: You do not have to be afraid to take a good look at your heart. Do you remember that you belong to Christ? Do you remember that nothing can ever separate you from the love of God? His plans are for our good, and our greatest good comes when God is our greatest love. To become aware of our sin and our idols is a good thing.

We cannot change what we will not acknowledge.
We must see our own sin, or we will not grow.

We might be saved for eternal life, but God wants even more. He wants to redeem this present life.

Here's the very best news: we are saved by grace, held by grace, and forgiven by grace. There is grace when God's light shines into our darkness. There is grace to help us name our idols. There is grace to confront our sin. And there will be grace to help us be redeemed. All is grace with God.

# READ AND MEDITATE

*TODAY'S READING: PSALMS 91—95*

**MY DAY 29 PRAYER FOR YOU**

*Father, help us run toward the truth inside. Help us see our idols. We've kept so much hidden in our hearts. Lord, call us into the light of Your grace, so we can be changed. So our sins can be forgiven. So our lives can be lived for Your glory, amen and amen*

# RESPOND IN PRAYER

Idolatry is seeking security and meaning in someone or something other than God.[10]
**A. R. BERNARD**

_____

_____

_____

_____

_____

_____

_____

_____

_____

_____

_____

DAY 30

# SO IDOLS CAN FALL

Last weekend, I was in a room of 4,000 women when the speaker asked, "If your family has a prodigal child, will you stand?" Our mouths dropped. I'm not sure what we expected, but from where I was sitting, about 80 percent of the room stood to their feet. Until that moment, I bet most of those women were feeling alone with their pain. Are you wondering if anyone else has the kind of burdens and problems you do? No matter what you are facing, you need to know you are not alone. There are Christian women all over this world who could stand with you. Humans have problems. Lots of them. There is no shame in having problems, or as I like to say, *It's hard to be a person.*

Today is about taking an honest look into our hearts. But before we do, just a quick word about the scope of our problems.

Some of the problems we face come from circumstances beyond our control. Some of our suffering is caused by the choices other people have made. Some of our problems come to us through natural disasters, accidents, disease, and more. As believers, we are called to live in a broken world where people suffer unspeakable pain. They endure things no person should ever have to endure and die in ways no one should ever die. Devastating injustice and harm happens when evil works through people, governments, authorities, and others.

Many times, you will be called to face problems that did not originate in your heart. The problem came to you, or fell on you, or attacked you by surprise. You did not cause it, nor did you encourage it. And yet, these problems have affected your heart. They left scars in your soul. They are yours to process and heal and be redeemed. But you are not alone. Many can stand with you, too. This world is fallen, and no one is exempt from its pain.

## WE ALL HAVE PROBLEMS, IDOLS, AND SIN

> They exchanged the truth about God for a lie and worshiped and served the creature rather than the Creator, who is blessed forever! Amen.
> **ROMANS 1:25**

There are a few ways we avoid dealing with our own sin:

**1. WE BELIEVE IF OUR CIRCUMSTANCES WOULD ONLY CHANGE, THEN WE'D BE FINE AND EVERYTHING WOULD BE OKAY. THE IDEAS ARE ENDLESS.**

If we could just get _____, then everything would change, and we would be happy.

*How would you fill in the blank above? Explain.*

**2. WE DON'T GET TO THE TRUTH OF OUR SIN BECAUSE WE SPIN OUR WHEELS JUST TRYING TO FIND AN EXTERNAL SOLUTION FOR OUR INTERNAL PROBLEM.**

- People get on my nerves—so I avoid them.
- I'm sad and rejected—I need someone to comfort me. Then another. And another.
- I hate my body—I need the right diet and exercise.
- My needs aren't being met—I have to find a way to get what I want.
- The kids don't respect me—So I scream and punish them, over and over.

**3. WE CAN SEE OUR PROBLEMS AS ORIGINATING SOMEWHERE ELSE BESIDES OUR OWN HEARTS. EVERYTHING AND EVERYBODY ELSE IS TO BLAME. WE'RE TRYING TO KEEP GOD AS OUR HIGHEST LOVE, BUT THE WORLD IS NOT COOPERATING.**

*Is any of this hitting a little too close to home? Explain.*

## UNCOVERING IDOLS

> Those who cling to worthless idols
> turn away from God's love for them.
> **JONAH 2:8 (NIV)**

Our study has been building up to this next section for a couple of days, so let's do the work today and really focus on any disorder we might find in our own hearts. We all have idols that need to fall.

It's possible to become blind to our own idols. Sometimes we are surprised by what we find. Would you ask the Holy Spirit to help you look into your own heart as honestly as you can?

*Some of the very best things in life become idols when they are turned into god-things. Place a check beside any of these good things that have the potential to become a god-thing in your own life.*

□ *Marriage*
□ *Children*
□ *Money*
□ *Beauty/ Appearance*
□ *Career*
□ *Church*
□ *Politics*

□ *A Good Cause*
□ *Dating*
□ *Friendships*
□ *A Possession*
□ *A Hobby*
□ *Rest/Comfort*
□ *Pleasure*
□ *Fitness*

□ *Affluence/ Status*
□ *Good Health*
□ *Sports*
□ *Success/ Achievements*

*Now consider a few more:*[11]

□ **ACCEPTANCE/ADMIRATION:** *Trying to earn someone's acceptance or approval.*

□ **HIGH STANDARDS:** *(Perfectionism) When you meet your high standard, you feel good; when you don't, you feel bad.*

□ **CONTROL AND THE PERFORMANCE OF OTHERS:** *Keeping account of what others must do/should do/didn't do.*

□ **HURT-FREE/PAIN-FREE LIFE:** *Avoiding the reality of problems. Believing there shouldn't be difficulties in my life. I don't want anything unsettling. I want peace.*

In *Counterfeit Gods,* Tim Keller instructs us concerning how to look for our idols:

Jesus says where your treasure is, is ultimately indicative of where your heart is. What do you treasure the most? If your house was on fire and you were running out, what would you take with you? That's indicative of your treasure. What is that person, thing, experience that you are most fearful of losing? Who or what do you love the most? What do you treasure? What is the source of your joy?

You can also look for that which you make sacrifices for. The Bible often uses the word *sacrifice* for worship, and the same is true for idolatry. Your time, where does it go? Your money, where does it go?[12]

Keller gives us the following four areas with questions to consider.[13]

**1. IMAGINATION AND WHAT WE FANTASIZE ABOUT.** The true god of your heart is what your thoughts effortlessly go to when there is nothing else demanding your attention.

*What do you enjoy daydreaming about?*

*What do you habitually think about to get joy and comfort in the privacy of your heart?*

**2. MONEY AND HOW WE SPEND IT.** Your money flows most effortlessly toward your heart's greatest love. In fact, the mark of an idol is that you spend too much money on it, and you must try to exercise self-control constantly. For most of us, however, we tend to over spend on clothing, or on our children, or on status symbols such as homes and cars. This reveals our idols.

> For where your treasure is, there your heart will be also.
> MATTHEW 6:21

*Where do you spend your money?*

> Corporate worship is designed to remind you that the world is ruled by a wise, gracious and capable King and he is not you.[14]
> PAUL DAVID TRIPP

*What do you most dream about being able to buy?*

**3. YOUR DAILY FUNCTIONAL SALVATION.** You may regularly go to a place of worship where you are a member. You may have a devout set of doctrinal beliefs. You may be trying very hard to believe and obey God. What are you really living for? What is your real—not just your professed—God? A good way to discern this is how you respond to unanswered prayers and frustrated hopes.

*What do you pray for? What do you work for? What are you really living for? What is the thing, that if you don't get it, you respond with explosive anger or deep despair—despair enough to die?*

**4. LIFE AND DEATH MATTERS AND HOW WE DEFINE THEM.** Look at your most uncontrollable emotions.

Just as a fisherman looking for fish knows to go where the water is roiling, look for your idols at the bottom of painful emotions, especially those that never seem to lift and that drive you to do things you know are wrong. If you are angry, ask yourself, *Is there something here too important to me, something I am telling myself I have to have at all costs?*

Are you so down on yourself because you have lost or failed at something which you think is a necessity when it is not? Are you overworking, driving yourself into the ground with frantic activity? Ask yourself, *Do I feel that I must have this thing to be fulfilled and significant?*

For the rest of today, will you let these questions and thoughts continue to percolate in your heart? Will you remain open to the prompting of the Holy Spirit concerning your idols? Will you respond to God's leading and guard against being misled?

# READ AND MEDITATE

*TODAY'S READING: PSALMS 96–100*

### MY DAY 30 PRAYER FOR YOU

*Father, I pray for the truth of our idols to be uncovered—the surface idols and our deeper idols. Help this one to search, uncover, and accept her true sin by Your grace. Father, speak mercifully to her. Instruct her with Your wisdom. Be near to her. In Jesus' name, amen.*

# RESPOND IN PRAYER

Prayer is the practice of drawing on the grace of God. Don't say, "I will endure this until I can get away and pray." Pray *now*—draw on the grace of God in your moment of need. Prayer is the most normal and useful thing; it is not simply a reflex action of your devotion to God. We are very slow to learn to draw on God's grace through prayer.[15]
**OSWALD CHAMBERS**

DAY 31

# SO YOU CAN TURN

It is never enough for us to intellectually recognize our idols. Now the question becomes, *What does God want us to do with our truth?*

*Has God revealed any idols to you? Potential idols? Surface? Deeper?*

I've said this several times, but it continues to bear repeating. Between salvation and heaven, we are on a journey of being redeemed. Each day, we are being made more and more into the image of Christ. This is a process. We will need a lifetime.

One of the most important things to remember on our journeys is to make every effort for our obedience to be quick. I am here to report it is such a painful, circular grind to willfully ignore the instruction of the Holy Spirit. If that's where you are, I can only tell you to just stop it. Really. Please, for yourself, and for all those who love you, get yourself out of all that misery. Stop ignoring God.

But how? I'm so thankful you asked.

## 1. BY BEING CONVICTED

I imagine these past few days you have experienced some conviction of sin or idols. I certainly have. We are convicted of our sin when we realize we're guilty of sin. The Bible says we know we are being convicted when we have a godly grief over our sin.

> For godly grief produces a repentance that leads to salvation
> without regret, whereas worldly grief produces death.
> **2 CORINTHIANS 7:10**

But there is a difference in godly grief and worldly grief. It's the little boy caught punching his sister under the dinner table. His dad instructs, "Say you're sorry." So out comes his worldly grief when, with fingers crossed behind his back, he begrudgingly mutters, "Sorry."

**Worldly grief** is "Sorry, not sorry." Or, "Sorry I got caught." Or, "Sorry seems like the right thing to say right now." It's remorse for all the wrong reasons. A counterfeit conviction.

**Godly grief** means God is the center of our attention. Godly grief is more than begging for the bad feelings to stop. Godly grief is begging for your heart to be changed.

Worldly grief will keep you in the same sin cycles over and over. Godly grief leads us to repentance—and that is when our heart can be changed. Worldly grief produces self-pity. Godly grief produces humility.

**When you "pull your emotions up by the roots," as it were, sometimes you will find your idols clinging to them.**[16]
**TIM KELLER**

*Do you recognize places in your own life where you only felt a worldly grief so you continued to repeat the same sin patterns with the same consequences over and over? Explain.*

*Do you have a godly grief over the sin or idols God has uncovered? Do you want God to change your heart? Why or why not?*

As the Holy Spirit convicts, ask Him also to help you see the sin beneath the sin.

### 2. BY CONFESSION

We can be convicted of our sin and know in our hearts we are guilty, yet still run away from confessing to the Lord that we have sinned against Him—and against His holiness. Essentially, we're deciding not to deal with it. To confess to God is to come clean, to own our thoughts, motives, and choices—to admit our sin. Read what Jesus said:

> You hypocrites! Well did Isaiah prophesy of you, when he said:
> "'This people honors me with their lips,
> but their heart is far from me;
> in vain do they worship me,
> teaching as doctrines the commandments of men.'"
> **MATTHEW 15:7-9**

Warning: Don't play with God on things like this. Live in your sin and stay far away from Him if you want to, but don't come into His presence, or the circle of chairs at your Bible study, and give a half-hearted confession. Don't pretend to reconcile with Him. I'm not saying bad things will happen to you or God's gonna get you. Scripture says it best:

*Read Galatians 6:7-9. According to verse 7, we should "not be deceived." Why?*

*How do we mock God with half-hearted confession?*

## 3. BY REPENTANCE

If you don't remember anything else, I hope you remember this: the next time you come face to face with your own sin, and you don't know what to do, I pray your heart starts yelling, "Repent! Repent!"

To repent is to turn away from your sin.

- It's about changing what you love.
- It is reordering the loves of your heart.
- You kill your love for your idol and return the focus of your love to God (Rom. 8:13).
- It's not a promise to change our affection. It's the actual work (that feels like work) to change.

We become followers of Jesus by repentance, and we continue to grow by repentance. The first time we repent by grace and every time after, it is the same grace that enables us. Growing up in Christ is a moment by moment, day after day, journey.

*Find these passages in your Bible and fill in the missing words.*

*_____ therefore, and turn back, that your sins may be blotted out (Acts 3:19).*

*For they themselves report . . . how you turned to God from _____ to serve the living and true God (1 Thess. 1:9).*

*If we say we have no sin, we _____ ourselves, and the truth is not in us. If we confess our sins, he is faithful and just to _____ us our sins and to cleanse us from all unrighteousness (1 John 1:8-9).*

Anytime you seek God's forgiveness, go to Him concerning your specifics. Sure, we can ask God for a general, *Lord, forgive me of my sins,* but honestly, you and I need to deal with our specific idols and our specific sins. *Lord, forgive my sharp tongue* is a specific request that gets to the truth of my sin. Besides, we don't just sweep through the room with a variety of miscellaneous sins in our pocket. We commit particular sins that are not the least bit vague or fuzzy.

*What uncovered idols do you need to seek God's forgiveness from?*

## 4. BY FAITHFULNESS

In our repentance, we reaffirm our faith in God to forgive us of our sins. Idols cannot simply be removed. We must also return God to His rightful place as our highest love. We set our whole hearts on Christ. God is faithful to forgive all who repent of their sins. He makes us clean, and He draws us closer. Knowing I am forgiven by a faithful God is pure and total freedom for me! There is no sweeter place to be. And when I have delayed to run to Him, I cannot understand how I forgot.

> How will we be redeemed? Faith and repentance.
> How will we grow into the image of Christ? Faith and repentance.
> How will our character bring glory to God? Faith and repentance.

I hope after five weeks in this study, you grasp the depth of those two words: faith and repentance.

## We are redeemed by faith and repentance— and we keep being redeemed by faith and repentance.

Do you want to live as a redeemed woman? *Faith and repentance.* Do you long for your character to be redeemed? *Faith and repentance.* A redeemed marriage? *Faith and repentance.* A redeemed story? *Faith and repentance.* The way of the redeemed is faith and repentance.

We could not return to God without Jesus Christ. But in Christ, we are redeemed.

# READ AND MEDITATE

*TODAY'S READING: PSALMS 101–104*

### MY DAY 31 PRAYER FOR YOU

*Oh Faithful Father, be our Redeemer. Restore this beautiful soul. Forgive all her sins. Bless her quick obedience. Comfort her grief. Redeem her heart. Redeem her character. Redeem her mistakes. Redeem her sin. Glorify Yourself with her faith and repentance. We love You. In Christ alone, amen.*

# RESPOND IN PRAYER

Don't believe everything you think. You cannot be trusted
to tell yourself the truth. Stay in The Word.[17]
**JERRY BRIDGES**

**DAY 32**

# READ, MEDITATE, & PRAY

For the essence of sin is man substituting himself for God (Genesis 3:1-7), while the essence of salvation is God substituting himself for man (2 Corinthians 5:21). Man asserts himself against God and puts himself where only God deserves to be; God sacrifices himself for man and puts himself where only man deserves to be.[18]
**JOHN STOTT**

## READ AND MEDITATE

*TODAY'S READING: PSALMS 105–107*

**MY DAY 32 PRAYER FOR YOU**

*Father, this beautiful soul is being redeemed and set free. Teach her to throw off the broken chains and live in the joy You have given. Free her from shame. Free her from guilt. Free her from her willfulness. In Jesus' precious name, amen.*

## RESPOND IN PRAYER

Repentance is both our path to forgiveness and the response that blooms from it.[19]
**SHE READS TRUTH**

_____

_____

_____

_____

_____

_____

_____

_____

_____

_____

_____

DAY 33

# READ, MEDITATE, & PRAY

How quickly we make good things, the supreme thing.

How quickly we worship the created instead of the Creator.

## READ AND MEDITATE

*TODAY'S READING: PSALMS 108–111*

**MY DAY 33 PRAYER FOR YOU**

*Father, do Your greater work in this sweet life. Reorder this heart so she lives every day as Your beloved. Restore peace and order to her home. Help her guide children from the grace and mercy You have given. Give her wisdom and joy in marriage. A readiness to serve when needed. A life well-lived for Your greater purpose and plan, amen and amen.*

## RESPOND IN PRAYER

Few things accelerate the peace process as much as humbly admitting our own wrongdoing and asking forgiveness.[20]
**LEE STROBEL**

# SESSION 6: VIEWER GUIDE

**REDEEMED FOR JOY**

> But the fruit of the Spirit is love, joy, peace, patience, kindness, goodness, faithfulness, gentleness, self-control; against such things there is no law.
> **GALATIANS 5:22-23**

> I am the true vine, and my Father is the vinedresser. Every branch in me that does not bear fruit he takes away, and every branch that does bear fruit he prunes.
> **JOHN 15:1-2a**

> I am the vine; you are the branches. Whoever abides in me and I in him, he it is that bears much fruit, for apart from me you can do nothing. If anyone does not abide in me he is thrown away like a branch and withers; and the branches are gathered, thrown into the fire, and burned. If you abide in me, and my words abide in you, ask whatever you wish, and it will be done for you. By this my Father is glorified, that you bear much fruit and so prove to be my disciples. As the Father has loved me, so have I loved you. Abide in my love. If you keep my commandments, you will abide in my love, just as I have kept my Father's commandments and abide in his love. These things I have spoken to you, that my joy may be in you, and that your joy may be full.
> **JOHN 15:5-11**

When you stay with Jesus, you become a woman who is growing in the _____ of _____.

The _____ is the _____ that you have been in the presence of God.

When our character is being redeemed, we are being redeemed for _____!

Video sessions available for purchase at *www.lifeway.com/redeemed*

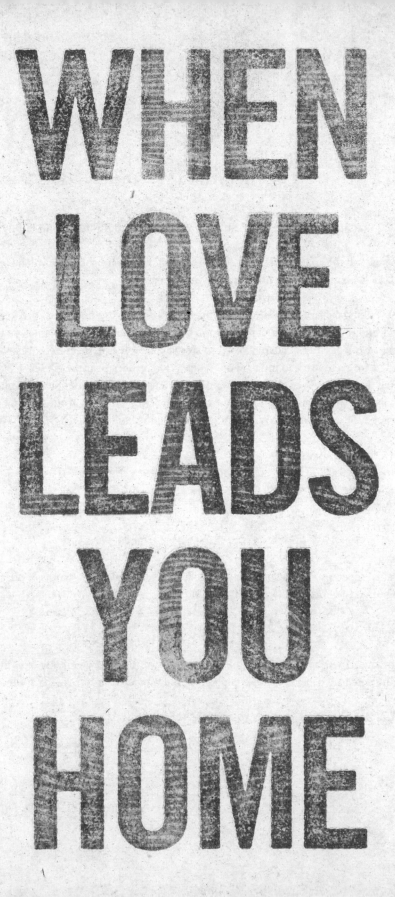

WHEN LOVE LEADS YOU HOME

**DAY 34**

# YOU WEAR HIS CROWN

The redeemed are changed people. And while we live, we continue being changed.

And one day, all the changing will be done. The work will be finished. We will be restored. We will be like Him. And we will be home. Redeemed.

As we're walking each other home, I want to encourage you. You do not have to keep living like the woman you have been. It is never too late to become what God wants you to be. You can be healed. You can change. You can start again. You can be set free. What a shame it would be for us to learn so much about redemption, yet not bear the evidence of being redeemed. In our last week together, I want us to focus on the kind of life a redeemed woman lives. If we are growing—if we are daily reordering our lives around God, if we are quick to obey, if we are quick to repent and restore faithfulness—there is *nothing* God can't do. And I mean nothing.

*Why do you think it's hard for most of us to grow in our faith? To let God change our lives?*

We've taken several weeks to spell it all out, to learn the foundational truths of our faith. But growing up in the Lord is not complicated.

We seek Him. Stay with Him. Return to Him.

Over and over, these simple instructions can bear powerful, God-glorifying fruit in our lives. Becoming a mature believer is not complicated. But mercy, it can sure be hard some days.

*What are some of the ways you can seek Him?*

*Stay with Him?*

*Return to Him?*

Will you open your Bible to Psalm 103? If you are reading through Psalms with us, you probably read this chapter last week. And if you did, then you already know David uses these 22 verses to celebrate our Redeemer. You may want to read the chapter all the way through, and then come back to verses 1-2.

*Who in the world is David talking to?*

If you said David is talking to himself, you'd be right! I once heard someone say about this chapter, "David is one soul, preaching to his own soul, with all his soul." In other words, he's giving himself a good talking to. He's giving himself a soul talk. The next 20 verses launch into the benefits (the mercies) of God, so David begins by reminding himself, these are the blessings he never wants to forget. These are the blessings to remember.

**Some Christians want enough of Christ to be identified with him but not enough to be seriously inconvenienced; they genuinely cling to basic Christian orthodoxy but do not want to engage in serious Bible study; they value moral probity, especially of the public sort, but do not engage in war against inner corruptions; they fret over the quality of the preacher's sermon but do not worry much over the quality of their own prayer life. Such Christians are content with mediocrity.[1]**
**D. A. CARSON**

Here's something to keep in mind as you are reading the Bible: whenever there is repetition, it is there for emphasis, so pay attention when you read the same phrases or words repeated.

*In Psalm 103:1-2, what phrase is repeated? (You see it again in verse 22.)*

To "bless" is more than to praise; it is to praise with affection and gratitude.[2]

*Do you forget how much God has blessed you? What makes you forget?*

*How do you remind yourself not to forget? Think of as many ways as you can. I promise you, whatever helps you remember is going to inspire somebody else!*

Don't miss verse 1, where David says, "bless his holy name!" I especially don't want you to miss the wonder and grace of this phrase.

Our Holy God forgives our sin. It is grace. And it is amazing.

*Verse 2 says, "Forget not all his _____."*

Now, a long train of mercies (benefits, blessings) begins with verse 3. But notice, in particular, the very first benefit.

*What is the first benefit in verse 3?*

I think you've already seen this with the Bible, but order is always important. The first benefit we receive from the Lord is forgiveness. Forgiveness must come first. Forgiveness is the thing that restores us to God, and no one can understand the benefits of God until she has been forgiven by God. We are blessed with the pardon of sin, and then we bless God for the pardon of sin.

Forgiveness never comes by itself. All the benefits of belonging to God always come with it. And who can receive the benefits of God? I think you remember; it's the same as who may be redeemed.

*Whosoever.* Whosoever believes.

*From verses 3-22, David gives this beautiful listing of benefits. There are many, but begin after our forgiveness in verse 3 and find five benefits that speak to your soul today. Write them below.*

*1.*

*2.*

*3.*

*4.*

*5.*

We aren't going to take the whole psalm line by line, but I want us to take one quick glance back at verses 4-5.

> Who redeems your life from the pit,
> who crowns you with steadfast love and mercy,
> who satisfies you with good
> so that your youth is renewed like the eagle's.
> **PSALM 103:4-5**

God redeems our life from the pit. HAL-LE-LU-JAH. Yes, He does! You are forgiven and restored to relationship with God. For some of you, the pit is a powerful memory of where you used to be. You remember exactly where you were. You know exactly when it happened. You understand exactly what God has delivered you from.

*What pit did God deliver you from? When did it happen? Or if you can't remember, what pit do you believe God saved you from?*

Only God could bring a woman up from the pit, and then give her a crown. This picture is so very powerful to us because it is exactly the opposite of what we deserve. We chose a crown to represent this Bible study because the crown is a symbol of redemption. In Psalm 103, the pit is exchanged for a crown. In Isaiah 61:3, a crown replaces a life of ashes.

When David says the redeemed are crowned with steadfast love and mercy, being crowned is the benefit, the blessing. In the same way a crown encircles the head, God encircles and surrounds the redeemed.

*According to verse 4, with what two things does God encircle the redeemed?*

*And one more time, who gets to wear a crown?*

Sinners who believe in Jesus wear the crown. *Whosoever.*

None of us would ever think ourselves worthy to wear a crown, especially one fashioned by the love and mercy of God. I believe that's why this picture is so very humbling—and why it makes us bow our heads to quote King David (Ps. 103:22): *Bless the Lord, O my soul! Thank You, Jesus, for redeeming my life from the pit.*

## Crowns for the Redeemed

**A Crown of Righteousness
(2 Tim. 4:7-8)**

**The Victor's Crown or
Imperishable Crown/
Wreath (1 Cor. 9:24-27)**

**An Unfading Crown of
Glory (1 Pet. 5:4)**

**A Crown of Rejoicing or
Boasting (1 Thess. 2:19)**

**The Crown of Life (Rev. 2:10)**

You shall be a crown of beauty in the hand of the Lord,
and a royal diadem in the hand of your God.
**ISAIAH 62:3**

# READ AND MEDITATE

*TODAY'S READING: PSALMS 112–118*

**MY DAY 34 PRAYER FOR YOU**

*Oh Father, remind this one not to forget. She is forgiven. She is
blessed. She does not live in a pit. She wears a crown. Bless the
Lord, O my soul, amen and amen.*

# RESPOND IN PRAYER

We must come to the Bible with the purpose of self-
exposure consciously in mind. I suspect not many people
make more than a token stab in that direction. It's
extremely hard work. It makes Bible study alternately
convicting and reassuring, painful and soothing,
puzzling and calming, and sometimes dull—but not
for long if our purpose is to see ourselves better.[3]
**LARRY CRABB**

DAY 35

# YOU WALK BY GRACE

Many of you know my backstory. Follower of Jesus. Called to ministry. Seminary graduate. Church staff. Married. Mom to four. Divorced. Single mom. Remarried. There's not time or a need to tell you the details of my backstory, but I can tell you this: It's not pretty. Many places in my life have been downright ugly and awful. This is not the life I'd want someone to imitate. Mine is not the story anyone ever hopes for.

I've done a lot of soul searching and God searching through the years. *Why couldn't I see what others could see? Did I miss God's leading? Was my sin to blame? Could I have done something to avoid all these years? Why didn't God stop me? Why doesn't God just expose all the injustice? Reveal all the liars? Stop all the wounding and suffering and pain?*

I'm a lot of years down the road now, and here are the honest answers I have so far.

*Why couldn't I see?* Immaturity. Self-centeredness. False sense of wisdom. Deception of this world. Lack of worldly understanding. Lack of mentoring. Unwilling to see. Narrow understanding of God's love.

*Did I miss God?* Maybe I did. Maybe I did not.

*Was it my sin?* I know I was not being punished for my sin. I do not believe our family's suffering is a direct consequence of my sin. My sinfulness fed my immaturity. It definitely contributed to my choices and my responses.

*Could I have avoided?* Absolutely. I made a free choice.

*Why didn't God stop me?* He made me free to choose, and I freely chose. Even though I belong to Him, we live in a fallen world, where there is evil. Even those who love God are deceived from the outside by the Accuser, and we are deceived from the inside by our own sin nature.

*Why does evil continue?* Because God is God, and I am not. Because God gave humanity the freedom to choose, and all creation fell. Because God is redeeming, but we are not yet home.

Maybe you are wondering why there is evil and suffering in this world. We've talked about it in previous weeks, but here's a reminder.

Evil and suffering occur because this world is still fallen. Jesus entered our world to ultimately take pain and suffering away. So Jesus paid the ultimate price for sin, suffering, and evil. The perfection of paradise was lost in the garden, but paradise will be regained in heaven. Everything in between is the story of being redeemed. The entire Bible is about God's decision to redeem. God sent His Son, Jesus, to save us from ourselves by taking on the punishment for our sins—so we don't have to.

*Why does suffering still occur on earth?* Because evil still exists. Jesus is still drawing people back into relationship with Him. But one day, evil and suffering will be no more because Jesus has already paid the price for it all.

There is still evil and suffering on earth because we are not yet home. Because the world is fallen. Because every human is born into sin. Because God delays returning so that more can know of His love (2 Pet. 3:1-9). Because God is God, and we are not.

Maybe you say, *But I don't understand?* I don't understand either.

> For now we see in a mirror dimly, but then face to face. Now I know in part; then I shall know fully, even as I have been fully known.
> **1 CORINTHIANS 13:12**

I trust God with what I only know in part. I trust that I only see through a mirror dimly. I know what God has done for me and I believe, with all my heart, that He will keep every promise He has made. In fact, I've staked my whole, entire life on His truth.

After living through the kind of pain and heartache best described as needless, unfair, ridiculous, and beyond all reasonable explanation. After watching my children suffer, and continue to suffer the stupid trauma and consequences of pain, you might ask if I still believe in God. My resounding answer is, *Yes, even more than I ever thought I could.*

And, after all this, there is one more thing I am absolutely sure of: the grace of God.

Some people say they have no regrets. Not me, I have many. I'd go back and redo so much if I could, but none of us can. Instead of rewinding our lives for a redo, the Lord instead, chooses to redeem. God saved my soul and promised me heaven, then left me on this earth with His forgiveness, His sympathy, and the comfort of His Holy Spirit. It is the grace of God by which we are redeemed. And it is the grace of God by which we continue to be redeemed.

As we walk by grace, our very lives are being redeemed. Our relationships. Our choices. Our wounds. Our pain. Our attitude. Our motives. Our broken stories. As Paul wrote,

But by the grace of God I am what I am, and his grace toward me
was not in vain. On the contrary, I worked harder than any of them,
though it was not I, but the grace of God that is with me.
**1 CORINTHIANS 15:10**

John Newton, writer of the hymn, "Amazing Grace," wrote of himself,

**I am not what I ought to be, I am not what I wish to be, I am not what
I hope to be; but, by the grace of God, I am not what I was.[4]**

The grace of God redeems.

From beginning to end, the Bible teaches us that the entire Christian life is dependent
on the grace of God. Find the following passages in your Bible and fill in any blanks below.

### 1. WE ARE REDEEMED AND SAVED BY GRACE ALONE.

*In him we have _____ through his blood,
the forgiveness of our trespasses, according to the riches of his
_____ (Eph. 1:7).*

*For by grace you have been _____ through
_____. And this is not your own doing, it is the _____ of
God (Eph. 2:8).*

### 2. WE CONTINUE TO EXPERIENCE THE GRACE OF GOD AS WE GROW.

*And now I commend _____ to God and to the word of his grace, which
is able to _____ you up and to give you the inheritance among all
those who are _____ (Acts 20:32).*

*But _____ in the grace and knowledge of our Lord and Savior Jesus
Christ (2 Pet. 3:18).*

### 3. WE ARE ENABLED FOR OUR CALLING BY GRACE.

*As each has received a _____, use it to _____ one another,
as good stewards of God's varied grace (1 Pet. 4:10).*

### 4. WE RECEIVE GOD'S GRACE FOR EVERY STRUGGLE WE FACE ON EARTH.

*And God is able to make all grace _____ to you, so that having
all sufficiency in _____ things at _____ times, you may abound in
every good work (2 Cor. 9:8).*

*But he gives _____ grace (Jas. 4:6).*

### 5. WE MUST COOPERATE WITH GOD TO CONTINUE EXPERIENCING HIS GRACE.

*We implore you on behalf of Christ, be _____ to God. For our sake he made him to be sin who knew no sin, so that in him we might become the righteousness of God. Working _____ with him, then, we appeal to you not to receive the grace of God in vain (2 Cor. 5:20b–6:1).*

Perhaps one of the best ways to know if you are truly being redeemed is to check your character for the marks of God's grace. Most of us can point to places and times where we have been recipients of His grace. But the spiritual growth of being redeemed means your character is being reshaped by grace. You are becoming more and more like what you received.

> For from his fullness we have all received, grace upon grace.
> JOHN 1:16

The way home is about becoming who you are in Christ—becoming to this world, the fullness of "grace upon grace." Grace in full means every part of you, everything that concerns you. Your character. The way you represent Jesus in the big ways and in the tiny, secret ways.

| | | | | |
|---|---|---|---|---|
| Countenance | Joy | Bitterness | Motives | Sacrifice |
| Judgment | Work | Concern | Emotions | Tone |
| Service | Grievances | Thoughts | Giving | Actions |
| Communication | Speech | Worship | Self-control | Laughter |

I can honestly tell you I would have never signed up for the story I have lived. Not even if you'd told me how the grace of God would make me better. The old, stubborn me would not have been convinced. She didn't know God the way I know Him now. But I can tell you this, like John Newton, I am not who I was. And, if there is anything better and sweeter about me, anything more like Jesus and less like the woman I have been, it is only because of the redeeming grace of God.

> God has and is redeeming my pain.
> God has and is redeeming my family.
> God has and is redeeming my heart.
> God has and is redeeming my story.

Some days I ran toward Him, wanting to cooperate with the grace that redeems. Other days, I pushed away, walked off, and stewed, focusing on my wounds. But I will tell you this, not one part of me was healed in my stewing. Everything that has been healed came by grace.

*Today, are you stewing in your problems, or are you cooperating with the grace of God? How are you seeing your character being redeemed? How?*

Can I give you some advice? Don't delay. I've learned some things the hardest possible ways. Every day lived apart from the grace of God is another day stolen by Satan and wasted. My beautiful Bible study friend, let the grace of God,

| | | |
|---|---|---|
| Redeem your struggles | Redeem your sin | Redeem your mistakes |
| Redeem your character | Redeem your home | Redeem your children |
| Redeem your marriage | Redeem your choices | Redeem your countenance |
| Redeem your decisions | Redeem your failures | Redeem your story. |

By grace, we will become better people than we've ever been.

# READ AND MEDITATE

*TODAY'S READING: PSALM 119*

**MY DAY 35 PRAYER FOR YOU**

*Father, I am so grateful to be overwhelmed by Your grace. Wherever this precious soul sits right now, will You pour out Your grace to overflowing? Will You comfort her, hold her, help her, restore her, redeem her? Will You tell her that sometimes cooperating means giving up on her own way, so she can trust Your way? May she rest in the gift of Your grace upon grace, amen.*

# RESPOND IN PRAYER

The Puritans . . . exhorted one another to "pray until you pray." Such advice is not to become an excuse for a new legalism . . . But in the Western world we urgently need this advice, for many of us in our praying are like nasty little boys who ring front doorbells and run away before anyone answers. Pray until you pray.[5]
**D.A. CARSON**

_____

_____

_____

_____

_____

DAY 36

# YOU LIVE IN HIS PRESENCE

A while back I told you about a conference I attended. By mid-afternoon on the first day of the conference, I had been diligently taking notes about the essence and parts of great storytelling. I thought the content and approach was brilliant, and I was totally into the whole thing—kind of like a math teacher learning a new way to explain calculus. I remember thinking, *Wow, this stuff will be so helpful to use when I'm teaching.*

The main speaker covered the elements of story and gave us examples of great stories. I was captivated. Just rocking along, learning so much, filling all the pages in my notebook. Then the speaker took a turn I didn't see coming. I guess there were about 2,000 other people in the room, but honestly, it felt like he loaded a Holy Spirit cannon and pointed it straight at me. I guess he said something like,

**Because God is the Creator of story, living a great story will involve these same elements. In the story God is writing for your life, you are the character with a journey to make. You must ask yourself these four questions:**

**1. Who are you?**
**2. What do you want?**
**3. What conflict must you engage?**
**4. What's the plan?**

I cannot remember the last time I immediately wanted to sob. I still don't know how I kept from bawling out loud right there in my seat. The tightness in my throat made me feel like I was going to choke. My tears fell faster than I could hide them. Caught off guard would be an understatement. *I thought it was a writing conference. What in the world?!*

I was actually doing fine until Question #2 grabbed me by the throat and made me cry. There was some kind of collision in my soul when I heard, *Angela, what do you want?*

> Was God asking, *Angela, what do you want Me to do for you?*
> Or was I pleading, *God, what do You want me to do for You?*
> Maybe it was God saying, *Angela, you get to choose, so just say what you want.*
> Me: *I'm afraid to choose. Can You just tell me what I want?*

Is it shocking to anyone that my children are also overthinker, philosopher, theologian types of people? God has to yank us back from ourselves or we'll lose friends and become hermit overthinkers who don't shower or get enough daylight. Ask me what I want for you. For your marriage. Your family. Your church. Your community. And I've got you covered. But what do I want? What do I want my story to be? Don't we believe in God and go along, growing in our faith, and God writes our story somehow?

I brought my notebook home and pondered that question from every angle. Finally, this argument with myself ensued. Thankfully, I believe the Holy Spirit was there to referee.

> *I can't even look at my wants. I have no idea what they are. I'm afraid of what I'll see. Besides, how can I ever trust what I want? I am a sinner. I am fallen. I have made a million mistakes. I have failed miserably. With my whole heart, mind, body, and soul, I want to bless God and love Him with my life. I'm afraid of looking at myself too long or too much. I'm afraid of doing things that make a big deal out of me.*

> *Do you trust that God is your Redeemer? I'm learning to trust Him, more and more. But I'm still so afraid of disordering my loves. Still afraid of missing God. Afraid of making my life about me.*

> *Do you trust the Redeemer to redeem? Do you trust the power of the Holy Spirit? Look intently at the One you trust. Keep your eyes on Him. Worship Him. Be a student of His Word. Imitate Him. Then, with your eyes on Your Father, say what you want. Angela, what do you want?*

That day at the conference and beyond, I have been humbled again by God's grace. In His presence, the redeemed can speak the truth of their desires. God is teaching me to trust Him afresh. To trust I am His redeemed. To trust the wiring He built inside of me. To trust the Holy Spirit to lead me. To trust that He still has more for me than I can ask, imagine, or hope.

My question for you is the same: *What do you want?*

God's whole story can be understood in terms of His presence. Man was removed from His presence by sin. From the garden to Egypt to the manger, God's purpose had to do with His presence.

In their sin, Adam and Eve hid themselves from the presence of God.

> And they heard the sound of the Lᴏʀᴅ God walking in the garden in
> the cool of the day, and the man and his wife hid themselves from
> the presence of the Lᴏʀᴅ God among the trees of the garden.
> **GENESIS 3:8**

God delivered the Israelites from Egypt to be with them.

> And they shall know that I am the Lᴏʀᴅ their God, who brought them out of
> the land of Egypt that I might dwell among them. I am the Lᴏʀᴅ their God.
> **EXODUS 29:46**

God sent His Son, Jesus, to be with us.

> And the Word became flesh and dwelt among us, and we have seen his
> glory, glory as of the only Son from the Father, full of grace and truth.
> **JOHN 1:14**

The plan of redemption restores all who believe to His presence. The redeemed live in the presence of God. We have access to God. We are hidden in Christ. We are indwelt by the Holy Spirit. What do you want in His presence? What are you striving for? Do you just want to go home? Want to be free? Want to be changed? Want to be happy?

*Take a few minutes to journal what comes into your heart.*

*Turn in your Bible to 2 Corinthians 3:17. Where is our freedom found?*

*Now look at 2 Corinthians 3:18. What is the believer looking at (beholding)? What is happening to the believer?*

*Find Isaiah 26:3. Who lives in perfect peace?*

*Now turn to Psalm 16:11. Where do we find joy?*

*For one last passage, fill in the missing words in Revelation 21:3-4.*

*And I heard a loud voice from the throne saying, "Behold, the dwelling place of God is with man. He will _____ with them, and they will be his people, and God himself will be with them as their God. He will wipe away every _____ from their eyes, and death shall be no more, neither shall there be _____, nor crying, nor pain anymore, for the former things have passed away."*

Separated from God's presence by sin. Restored to God's presence by Jesus. On our way home where we shall dwell with Him forever.

*Where will you find freedom?* In His presence.
*Where will you be changed?* In His presence.
*Where is your peace?* In His presence.
*Your joy?* In His presence.

May I encourage you as God has encouraged me? If we strive for anything on earth, let us strive to be in His presence. In God's presence, we can trust Him to be greater. We say what we want. We can name our fears. We can confront our sin.

In His presence, we are being redeemed.

# READ AND MEDITATE

*TODAY'S READING: PSALMS 120–124*

**MY DAY 36 PRAYER FOR YOU**

*Father, may Your presence be our first priority. Teach this one to live in Your presence. Run back to Your presence. Yearn for Your presence. Comfort her there. Restore her. Change her. Give her joy. In Jesus' name, amen.*

# RESPOND IN PRAYER

The Psalms train us to pray with others who have prayed, and are praying: put our knees on the level with other bent knees; lift our hands in concert with other lifted hands; join our voices in lament and praise with other voices who weep and laugh. The primary use of prayer is not for expressing ourselves, but in becoming ourselves.[6]
**EUGENE H. PETERSON**

DAY 37

# YOU ARE LEARNING TO GROW

We're just about to wind this study down, but I'm praying God is doing just the opposite in your soul. I'm asking Him to keep winding you up! There is so much more of this life to be lived. What if we truly begin living like our chains are broken? With the assurance of forgiveness? With new eyes to see? With a renewed commitment to prayer and God's Word? What if we have seen God answer so many prayers that we'll never stop praying again? What if reading through Psalms has become one of the sweetest parts of each day?

Redeemed people begin living every day better than before, not because we have new strategies or new plans, but because we're being changed by God. Because we've learned to trust His grace.

> We long to be transformed.
> We long for His presence.
> We long to be like Him.
> We long to bring Him glory.

I've been stumbling and bumbling along writing this study. Sort of a theology class. Sort of discipleship. Sort of a topical study. Sort of small group sharing. Sort of a pep rally. I've worried there's not enough Bible teaching. Not enough theology learned. Not enough personal application. Not enough stories. It's not funny enough. It's not clear enough. It's too detailed. Too elementary. Too seminary. Too confusing. You name it, the Accuser brought it to mind.

He has taught me so much about my own sin and all sin in general. Most all of it, big and small, is rooted in pride. And if I trace my fears, most of them lead back to my pride too.

I've been learning not to fear searching for what my soul wants and desires. If I seek the presence of God, stay in the presence of God, and return to the presence of God, all that concerns me is being redeemed—including my wants.

*How about you? Where are you learning? Processing? Growing?*

God isn't interested in a bunch of us learning to manage our struggles in a more godly way. He wants us to understand we've been cured! We are free. The victory is certain. Our future is secure.

*Do you see the difference in managing a certain struggle and learning to live as a free woman? What would that look like in your life?*

Have you ever heard someone talk about FOMO (fear of missing out) or tag their Instagram #YOLO (you only live once)? Those acronyms don't apply to the redeemed. Are you kidding me? We are not going to miss anything. If I don't get to visit every continent in this lifetime, I'm absolutely sure my future includes the new heavens and new earth. And, we don't just live once, so we better hurry and cram in everything. We live here and now, and we will live for eternity.

*Describe the person who lives with a constant FOMO.*

*Now describe the person who lives assured that God's eternity includes all.*

Thankfully, God in His grace is not impatient with our humanity. Depending on how you count it, the Old Testament says at least 196 times, *the steadfast love of the Lord never ends.* Why does God use repetition in the Bible? To emphasize His point! He's not mad that we're slow runners sometimes. The steadfast love of the Lord never ends.

You and I can be redeemed, yet not steadily growing in all God has called us to become. As a matter of fact, we can just lose sight of the goal. Lose our sense of awareness. Forget to remember that *I need to keep growing in the Lord!*

We all still need to be changed. Our focus will continually need readjusting. We have new potential just waiting to be set free, but new potential requires continued spiritual growth. We realize new potential as we push deeper into our commitment to grow in godliness. The Bible warns about one of the ways it's easy to become sidetracked.

> The fear of man lays a snare,
> but whoever trusts in the LORD is safe.
> **PROVERBS 29:25**

They say whatever you think you need the most is the thing that eventually controls you. Many Christians are kept from their new potential in Christ because the fear of man controls our hearts. And we can stir that thing around with enough spiritual words to almost make our choices seem right.

> We don't parent in strength because we fear not being loved or liked.
> We over commit in a million ways, pleasing people we're afraid to disappoint.
> We hyper-focus on ways to succeed because our fear of man is like a peer pressure to keep up.
> We make people more important to please than God.
> The opinions of others guide our choices. Our spending. Our self-talk. Our white lies. Our envy.
> Co-dependency is fearing we have to be attached to a certain person.

Like a fatal flaw, the fear of man is sneaky, weaving itself through our humanity. The ways we allow others to control and guide our lives can be huge or subtle, but every time we worry more about pleasing man more than pleasing God, we are sacrificing the potential growth, potential fruit, and potential freedom God wants to bring to our lives.

*What ways do you see the fear of man manifest in your life?*

Almost every secular approach that tries to help people with their fear of man tells us to learn to love ourselves. *Focus on yourself. Make time for yourself a priority.* None of those ideas are bad in and of themselves, but they are not the answers. The Bible has a different answer. It says the fear of the Lord is the way to deal with our fear of man, trusting in God above everything else.

> The end of the matter; all has been heard. Fear God and keep
> his commandments, for this is the whole duty of man.
> **ECCLESIASTES 12.13**

To fear the Lord means putting God in His rightful place in our lives. That means God must become bigger than people.[7]

*Look at some of the ways the Bible describes the fear of the Lord. Beside each passage, write the benefit given to those who fear God.*

_____ *The friendship of the LORD is for those who fear him, and he makes known to them his covenant (Ps. 25:14).*

_____ *The angel of the LORD encamps around those who fear him, and delivers them (Ps. 34:7).*

_____ *The fear of the LORD is the beginning of knowledge; fools despise wisdom and instruction (Prov. 1:7).*

_____ *The fear of the LORD is the beginning of wisdom, and the knowledge of the Holy One is insight (Prov. 9:10).*

_____ *The fear of the LORD prolongs life, but the years of the wicked will be short (Prov. 10:27).*

_____ *In the fear of the LORD one has strong confidence, and his children will have a refuge (Prov. 14:26).*

_____ *The fear of the LORD is a fountain of life, that one may turn away from the snares of death (Prov. 14:27).*

_____ *The fear of the LORD leads to life, and whoever has it rests satisfied; he will not be visited by harm (Prov. 19:23).*

_____ *Let not your heart envy sinners, but continue in the fear of the LORD all the day (Prov. 23:17).*

The redeemed are learning to live what we have become in Christ. We are new people with a new life, new hope, and new potential. We learn to grow into what we can be: a new creation with brand new potential.

**Sanctification is like a clumsy, slow walk rather than a light with that we turn from off to on. But by God's grace we grow.[8] ED WELCH**

Praise God, the life of the redeemed has already been granted more new potential than we can fathom! We are the people who fear the Lord. And we are the people still learning to fear the Lord. I pray you won't spend one more day beating yourself up. Not one more day shame-talking your soul. We've all done enough of that. Let's stop now, and help each other stop. Let's grow as the redeemed.

New potential can be a slow journey of grace, one day, then another day, learning and remembering and being reminded. It is checking and rechecking the order of our heart's loves. Fearing the Lord by moving Him back to first place. Then, moving Him back there again. And then again.

But let's try. And let's cheer for one another. And let's carry one another. Because the steadfast love of the Lord never ends, we can be changed. We will be changed.

# READ AND MEDITATE

*TODAY'S READING: PSALMS 125–135*

**MY DAY 37 PRAYER FOR YOU**

*Lord, God, You have given us more than we can ever realize. But for this dear one, Father, will You give her a glimpse today? Will You let her catch a vision of the woman You see? The new potential just waiting for her? God will You grow her up and strengthen her godly fear, so any fear of man falls away? Be near to her. Make Your glory so easy for her to see. Bless her and bless her and bless her. In Jesus' name, amen.*

# RESPOND IN PRAYER

Presumptuous prayer speaks to God without first listening to him. It obsessively anxiously, or pretentiously multiplies human words to God, but with, at best, a distracted, indifferent, or fitful interest in God's words to us. But God speaks to us before we speak to him. If we pray without listening, we pray out of context.[9]
**EUGENE H. PETERSON**

DAY 38

# YOU ARE READY. THE DAY IS TODAY. LET'S GO.

My personal commitment to live every day as God's redeemed is passionate and intense, and many days probably a little overwhelming to the people who love me. It's the kind of drive that packs my bags and sends me out many weekends, begging God to make my words into a tool He can use. It's that same commitment that pushes me to study and hibernate and rewrite like crazy, pleading for the kind of writing that becomes a vessel of God's work.

Here is the greatest threat to everything I do.

My talk is never ready. My words are never good enough. My stories are never as good as I think they could be. I've never studied enough. My timing isn't all figured out. My pacing. My outlines. And oh mercy, I'm just getting started. The bomb drops when I declare my soul is not ready. I never wake up thinking, *Yeah baby, bring it on, I'm ready!* It's usually more like, *Lord, just get it over with. Put us all out of my misery.*

Left to my natural inclinations, my go-to responses, and my old nature settings, I'd take forever to get ready if you'd let me. We are *being* redeemed. God is calling us to live and go and become and love and serve, right in the middle of our not-ready-yet fears.

*What is on your mental list of the ways you're not ready for something God has called you to do?*

We talked about the Great Commission earlier, but let's take this last day of study to dive in and answer the following questions.

*Read Matthew 4:12-16. According to verse 12, where did the ministry of Jesus' good news (gospel) begin?*

Verses 15-16 quote the prophet Isaiah. Jesus declared He is the long-awaited fulfillment of Isaiah's prophecy.

*From verse 16, fill in the blanks: The people dwelling in darkness have
seen a great light, and for those dwelling in the region and shadow of
death, on them a _____ has _____.*

Galilee is the place where Jesus proclaimed that He is the light breaking the darkness.
He is the prophesied Messiah. He is the hope of the world.

*Now, turn to Matthew 10:5-7 and read the first commissioning of Jesus'
disciples. In verse 5, Jesus told the disciples not to go two places. What
are they?*

*In verse 6, He instructed them only to go to one specific group of people.
Who are they?*

*The Great Commission passage comes at the end of Matthew's Gospel and
at the end of Jesus' earthy ministry. With these final words, Jesus made
three important declarations. Underline them in the passage below.*

[16] Now the eleven disciples went to Galilee, to the mountain to which Jesus
had directed them. [17] And when they saw him they worshiped him, but
some doubted. [18] And Jesus came and said to them, "All authority in heaven
and on earth has been given to me. [19] Go therefore and make disciples of
all nations, baptizing them in the name of the Father and of the Son and
of the Holy Spirit, [20] teaching them to observe all that I have commanded
you. And behold, I am with you always, to the end of the age."
**MATTHEW 28:16-20**

*Who is Jesus talking to in this passage?*

*Where does this final scene take place?*

*What two things do they do when the disciples see Jesus?*

The Gospel of Matthew ends in the very same place it begins—Galilee. But this second commissioning of the disciples is different. Because Jesus had already appeared to the disciples,
they were not doubting His resurrection, but they may have been doubting if the One they
were seeing on that mountain was actually the real Jesus. I love that the disciples worshiped

and some even worshiped with their doubts. Jesus' next words are full of great meaning and instruction, but all doubt was relieved as Jesus began to speak. He surely reassured them and strengthened them for their calling.

### 1. A DECLARATION OF AUTHORITY

*Who has been given "all authority in heaven and on earth" (v. 18)?*

*What is the "therefore" in verse 19 there for?*

Jesus has been given authority by the will of God to issue the next declaration we know as the Great Commission. The only thing that qualifies us to "go . . . make disciples" is that Jesus Christ has been given "all authority in heaven and on earth." We are in Him, and He is in us.

### 2. A DECLARATION OF COMMISSION

*From verse 19, fill in the blanks: Go therefore and make _____ of all _____.*

When we compare Matthew 10 and Matthew 28, we see the restriction to go to Israel only has been lifted. The good news of Jesus is now extended to all nations and all people. Light breaks into the darkness of the whole world. Hope has come for all.

The main Greek verb in this passage is, *mathēteúsō,* and means *making disciples.*

**Mathēteúō means not only to learn, but to become attached to one's teacher and to become his follower in doctrine and conduct of life.[10]**

The other three verbs in the commission (*going, baptizing,* and *teaching*) are all participles, which means they relate to the main verb. *The Believer's Bible* gives this paraphrase:

**As you go forth, call people everywhere to become disciples, which will involve both baptizing them into God's community and summoning them to embody my teaching in their lives.[11]**

You and I are called to go.

### 3. A DECLARATION OF ASSURANCE

*Turn back to Matthew 1:23. What does the name "Immanuel" mean?*

At the beginning of Matthew, Jesus was named "God with us." At the end of Matthew, Jesus promised He will continue to be with us.

God does not redeem us to make us happy. Nor does He keep redeeming us just to make us better. God is on mission in this world doing two things: (1) to reach the lost with the news of His steadfast love, and (2) to change the found into the image of His Son.

Does God's plan make your life better? You bet it does. When the created live as the Creator intended, it's the best thing ever. In fact, better than anything you could ever imagine, ask, or hope for.

God redeems us to join His mission on earth. And everywhere God is working in this world, He's using a bunch of not-yet-ready, being-redeemed kind of people. The kind of people who don't have enough strength on their own. People who've been separated from God by their sin. Wounded people who've wounded others. People who forget what they've been given and need to be reminded again. People who still need forgiveness. Still need to change. People who truly aren't ready.

Why would God send people like you and me into the world to do His work and then be with us always? For the praise of His glorious grace.

# READ AND MEDITATE

*TODAY'S READING: PSALMS 136–139*

**MY DAY 38 PRAYER FOR YOU**

*Father, may Your grace to us be Your praise. May Your forgiveness make Your name great. Will You send this one on Your mission? Remind her You're always with her. For Your praise and Your glory, amen and amen.*

# RESPOND IN PRAYER

The Psalms were not prayed by people trying to understand themselves. They are not the record of people searching for the meaning of life. They were prayed by people who understood that God had everything to do with them. God, not their feelings, was the center. God, not their souls, was the issue. God, not the meaning of life, was critical.[12]
**EUGENE H. PETERSON**

**DAY 39**

# READ, MEDITATE, & PRAY

Behold, I am with you always, to the end of the age.
**MATTHEW 28:20b**

## READ AND MEDITATE

*TODAY'S READING: PSALMS 140–145*

**MY DAY 39 PRAYER FOR YOU**

*Father, for this dear redeemed soul, I ask for new passion and new courage. Do not let her keep Your great love to herself. Let the truth pour from her heart, through her words, her eyes, and her life. Remind her over and over of what You have done for her. Because of Jesus, our Redeemer, amen.*

## RESPOND IN PRAYER

A love that can never be fathomed; A life that can never die; A righteousness
that can never be tarnished; A peace that can never be understood;
A rest that can never be disturbed; A joy that can never be diminished;
A hope that can never be disappointed; A glory that can never be clouded;
A light that can never be darkened; A happiness that can never be interrupted;
A strength that can never be enfeebled; A purity that can never be defiled;
A beauty that can never be marred; A wisdom that can never be baffled;
Resources that can never be exhausted.[13]
**ANONYMOUS**

_____

_____

_____

_____

_____

_____

_____

# DAY 40

# READ, MEDITATE, & PRAY

This life therefore is not righteousness, but growth in righteousness, not health, but healing, not being but becoming, not rest but exercise. We are not yet what we shall be, but we are growing toward it, the process is not yet finished, but it is going on, this is not the end, but it is the road. All does not yet gleam in glory, but all is being purified.[14]
**MARTIN LUTHER**

## READ AND MEDITATE

*TODAY'S READING: PSALMS 146–150*

**MY DAY 40 PRAYER FOR YOU**

*Redeemer, Father, Savior and Lord, be glorified today. Be exalted today. May Your presence for this one be thick and sweet and the place she always longs to be. Keep her safe, wrapped in the robes of Your glory. Keep her tender, filled with the power of the Holy Spirit. Keep redeeming her life and her relationships and her very soul. May she live for Your Name. Serve in Your Name. Love in Your name. Because no name is sweeter, in Jesus' name we pray, amen.*

## RESPOND IN PRAYER

I assume the Spirit is always whispering,"Abba," to God's children, assuring them that they are safe in His care. And he is continually calling them to become what God saved them to be, solid people, indestructibly alive, hurting perhaps, but consumed with pleasing the Father.[15]
**LARRY CRABB**

# SESSION 7: VIEWER GUIDE

**REDEEMED FOR LOVE**

> For this reason I bow my knees before the Father, from whom every family in heaven and on earth is named, that according to the riches of his glory he may grant you to be strengthened with power through his Spirit in your inner being, so that Christ may dwell in your hearts through faith—that you, being rooted and grounded in love, may have strength to comprehend with all the saints what is the breadth and length and height and depth, and to know the love of Christ that surpasses knowledge, that you may be filled with all the fullness of God.
> **EPHESIANS 3:14-19**

If you are _____ and _____ in the Word of God, you've got the _____ to fight in the dark.

Video sessions available for purchase
at *www.lifeway.com/redeemed*

# ENDNOTES

## WEEK 1

1. Augustine, *The City of God: The Words of Saint Augustine, A Translation for the 21st Century* (New York: New City Press, 2012), 304.
2. Hudson Taylor, quoted by Thomas E. Stephens, "One of Hudson Taylor's Helpers," in *Good News for Russia: A Series of Addresses,* ed Jesse Wendell Brooks (Chicago: The Bible Institute Colportage Association, Moody Press, 1918), 32.
3. Carpenter, E. E., & Comfort, P. W. In *Holman Treasury of Key Bible Words: 200 Greek and 200 Hebrew Words Explained and Defined* (Nashville, TN: Broadman & Holman Publishers, 2000), 146.
4. Flannery O'Connor, *A Prayer Journal* (New York: Farrar, Straus, 2013), 3. Quoted in Tim Keller's *Prayer* (New York: Penguin Books, 2016), 11.
5. I attribute this phrasing to Dr. Norman Geisler.
6. Timothy Keller, *Prayer,* 50
7. As I was preparing this week of lessons, my pastor, Don Miller, at Westover Church in Greensboro, NC, preached from this passage on the first Sunday of Advent, 2015. In his sermon, Pastor Don vividly painted the picture of the garden in "Scene One," and the sadness of Adam and Eve's fate in "Scene Two." In today's session, I am using his depiction of these juxtaposed scenes with regard to God's plan for redemption.
8. Ibid.

## WEEK 2

1. Paul E. Miller, *A Praying Life, Connecting With God in a Distracting World,* Colorado Springs, CO: NavPress, 2009), 20.
2. C.S. Lewis. *The Screwtape Letters* (New York: HarperSanFrancisco, 2001), ix.
3. Wayne Grudem, *Bible Doctrine: Essential Teachings of the Christian Faith* (Grand Rapids: Zondervan, 1999), 168.

4. C.S. Lewis, *Mere Christianity,* Revised ed. (New York: HarperOne, 2001), 121.
5. C.S. Lewis, *God in the Dock: Answers to Questions on Christianity* (Grand Rapids: Wm B. Eerdmans Publishing Company, 1970), 46.
6. Watchman Nee, *What Shall This Man Do?* (London: Victory Press, 1961), 96.
7. W. A. Elwell and Philip Comfort, *Tyndale Bible Dictionary* (Wheaton, IL: Tyndale House Publishers, 2001), 474.
8. Robert L. (Bob)Deffinbaugh, "5. The Fall of Man in God's Perfect Plan," published May 17, 2004. Available online at *https://bible.org/seriespage/5-fall-man-gods-perfect-plan.* Accessed 27 May 2016.
9. C.H. Spurgeon, "Sermon (No. 1051): Golden Bowls Full Of Incense Delivered" in *The Power of Prayer in a Believer's Life* (Lynwood: WA: Emerald Books, 1993), 91.
10. O. Palmer Robertson, "The Christ of the Covenants,. Available online at *www.colsoncenter.org/the-center/columns/indepth/14937-introduction-to-the-covenants.* Accessed 27 May 2016.
11. Ibid.
12. Paul E. Miller, *A Praying Life,* 21
13. Ibid., 23.
14. Ibid.

## WEEK 3

1. "Charles R. Swindoll>Quotes," GoodReads.com. Accessed 31 May 2016. Available at *www.goodreads.com.*
2. John Eldredge, *Moving Mountains* (Nashville: Thomas Nelson, 2016), 11.
3. C.H. Spurgeon, "How to Read the Bible: A Sermon (No. 1503)," The Spurgeon Archive. Accessed 31 May 2016. Available at *www.spurgeon.org.*
4. Norman L. Geisler, *Systematic Theology: In One Volume* (Ada, MI: Bethany House, 2011), 800.

5. John MacArthur, *New Testament Commentary: Matthew 1-7* (Chicago: Moody Press, 1985), 255.

6. Philip Yancey, *Prayer: Does It Make A Difference?* (Grand Rapids: Zondervan, 2006), 17.

7. Norman L. Geisler, *A Popular Survey of the New Testament* (Grand Rapids: Baker Books, 2007), chapter 1, ebook edition.

8. W. A. Elwell and B. J. Beitzel, *Baker Encyclopedia of the Bible* (Grand Rapids, MI: Baker Book House, 1988), 746.

9. John Murray, *Redemption Accomplished and Applied* (Grand Rapids: Wm. B. Eerdmans Publishing, 2015), ebook ed.

10. Yancey, *Prayer: Does It Make a Difference?*, 26.

11. Spiros Zodhiates, ed., *The Complete Word Study Dictionary: New Testament,* (Chattanooga, TN: AMG Publishers, 2000), 1160.

12. Louw, J. P., & Nida, E. A. (1996). *Greek-English lexicon of the New Testament: based on semantic domains* (electronic ed. of the 2nd edition., Vol. 1, p. 375). New York: United Bible Societies.

13. Zodhiates, *The Complete Word Study Dictionary: New Testament,* 1162.

14. Ibid., 1161.

15. John Murray, *Redemption; Accomplished and Applied*, 111-112.

16. Tim Keller, Twitter post, May 19, 2014, 10:05 a.m., *https://twitter.com/timkellernyc.*

17. "Augustine of Hippo>Quotes," GoodReads.com. Accessed 31 May 2016. Available at *www.goodreads.com.*

18. Quoted in *Jonathan Edwards and the Bible* by Robert E. Brown (Bloomington: Indiana University Press, 2002), 3.

19. C.H. Spurgeon, Spurgeon's Sermons on Prayer (Peabody, MA: Hendrickson Publishers, 2007), 30.

**WEEK 4**

1. Donald Miller, "How To Tell a Story," 2015 Story Conference handout, 34.

2. "Charles Haddon Spurgeon>Quotes," GoodReads.com. Accessed 31 May 2016. Available at *www.goodreads.com.*

3. Graham Kendrick, *Worship* (Eastbourne: Kingsway Publications, 1984), 26.

4. Zodhiates, *The Complete Word Study Dictionary: New Testament,* 1233.

5. Tim Keller, Main Sessions, The Evangelists Conference 2007, *www.evangelists-conference.org.uk/2007.php*

6. John Eldredge, *Moving Mountains,* 8.

7. David Garland, *New American Commentary, Volume 29: 2 Corinthians* (Nashville: B&H Publishers, 1999), 286.

8. Ibid., 287.

9. J. Philip Arthur, *Strength in Weakness: 2 Corinthians Simply Explained (Welwyn Commentary Series)* (Welwyn Garden City: EP Books, 2004), ebook edition.

10. Garland, *New American Commentary,* 287.

11. "Dwight L. Moody>Quotes," GoodReads.com. Accessed 31 May 2016. Available at *www.goodreads.com.*

12. Yancey, *Prayer: Does It Make A Difference?,* 44.

13. C.H. Spurgeon, *Spurgeon Gold,* compiled by Ray Comfort (Alachua, FL: Bridge-Logos, 2005), 52.

14. Bob Goff, Twitter post, February 16, 2015, 7:10 p.m., *https://twitter.com/bobgoff.*

15. "Corrie ten Boom>Quotes," GoodReads.com. Accessed 31 May 2016. Available at *www.goodreads.com.*

16. "Oswald Chambers>Quotes," GoodReads.com. Accessed 31 May 2016. Available at *www.goodreads.com.*

17. Elisabeth Elliot, *A Lamp Unto My Feet* (Ventura, CA: Regal, 2004), 34.

**WEEK 5**

1. John Donne, *Selections from the Works of John Donne* (Oxford: D.A. Talboys, 1840), 19.

2. G. W. Hansen, *The Letter to the Philippians* (Grand Rapids, MI: William B. Eerdmans Publishing Company, 2009), 177.

3. C. S. Lewis, *The Screwtape Letters* (New York: HarperOne, 2001), 60-61.

4. Jerry Bridges, *The Pursuit of Holiness* (Colorado Springs: NavPress, 1996), 57.

5. Augustine of Hippo, *Selections from Confessions and Other Essential Writings* Woodstock: VT: Skylight Paths Publishing, 2010), 99.

6. Timothy Keller, *Counterfeit Gods: The Empty Promises of Money, Sex, and Power, and the Only Hope That Matters* (New York: Dutton, 2009), xix.

7. Ibid., 64-66.

8. John Calvin, *Institutes of the Christian Religion,* ed. John T. McNeill (Philadelphia, PA: Westminster Press, 1060), 108.

9. Ibid.

10. A. R. Bernard, Twitter post, July 13, 2013, 7:01 a.m., h*ttps://twitter.com/ arbernard.*

11. Some of these prompts are inspired by a handout called "Identifying Personal Idols" by Grace Fellowship Church, Florence, KY.

12. Timothy Keller, *Counterfeit Gods,* epilogue

13. Ibid.

14. Paul David Tripp, Twitter post, April 6, 2014, 5:37 a.m., *https://twitter.com/ paultripp.*

15. Oswald Chambers, *My Utmost for His Highest: Updated* (Grand Rapids: Discovery House, 2010), June 26.

16. Timothy Keller, *Counterfeit Gods.*

17. Jerry Bridges, *The Great Exchange* (Wheaton, IL: Crossway, 2007).

18. John Stott, *The Cross of Christ* (Downers Grove: Inter Varsity Press, 1986), 160.

19. Marcie Porterfield , "Forgiveness and Repentance," She Reads Truth. Accessed 1 June 2016. Available at *http://shereadstruth.com/.*

20. Lee Strobel, *God's Outrageous Claims* (Grand Rapids: Zondervan, January 2009), epub.

**WEEK 6**

1. D.A. Carson, *A Call to Spiritual Reformation* (Grand Rapids: Baker Academic, 1992), 121.

2. Spence-Jones, H.D.M., *Psalms* (London: Funk & Wagnalls, 1909), 382.

3. "Larry Crabb>Quotes," GoodReads.com. Accessed 1 June 2016. Available at *www. goodreads.com.*

4. "John Newton>Quotes," GoodReads.com. Accessed 1 June 2016. Available at *www. goodreads.com.*

5. D.A. Carson, *A Call to Spiritual Reformation,* 37.

6. Eugene Peterson, *Answering God* (New York: HarperOne, 1991), 19.

7. Edward T. Welch, *When People Are Big, And God Is Small* (Phillipsburg, NJ: Reformed Publishing Company, 1997), 192.

8. Ibid.

9. Eugene Peterson, *Answering God,* 53.

10. Zodhiates, *The Complete Word Study Dictionary: New Testament,* 936 .

11. R. B. Gardner, *Matthew* (Scottdale, PA: Herald Press, 1991), 402.

12. Eugene H. Peterson, *Answering God,* 14.

13. P. L. Tan, *Encyclopedia of 7700 Illustrations: Signs of the Times* (Garland, TX: Bible Communications, Inc., 1996), 516-517.

14. Martin Luther>Quotes," GoodReads.com. Accessed 1 June 2016. Available at *www. goodreads.com.*

15. "Larry Crabb>Quotes," GoodReads.com. Accessed 1 June 2016. Available at *www. goodreads.com.*

# LEADER GUIDE

Thank you for leading the study of *Redeemed*. This brief leader guide offers some ideas, but I urge you to rely on the Holy Spirit for true guidance. These are only suggestions.

Let's start with the order of events in group study: You will first study the week of print material on a topic, then watch the video, and finally share in a small group. For the first week your group will watch the Session 1 video and do some basic group building. Then members will study Week 1 in preparation for Session 2.

To prepare for leading each week, complete the study and preview the video. Set up the meeting room, including the necessary equipment. The suggested questions in this leader guide come from the week's personal study or build upon the week's personal study. They are intended to be discussion starters.

## SESSION 1

Use the first session to build fellowship in your group. Familiarize yourself with the contents of the study. Preview the study for the members, so they will know what is expected each week. Watch the Session 1 video and ask members what they hope to gain from your time together. (Note: In all other sessions, the Viewer Guide is found after the personal study.) Here are some additional suggestions:

*1. Invite the women introduce and share something about themselves.*

*2. Direct members to the table of contents on page 3. Ask which topics they are eager to study and which they are hesitant about.*

*3. Encourage women to be honest and maintain absolute confidentiality, as you will be talking about sensitive topics.*

*4. Be sure each woman gets a copy of* Redeemed: Grace to Live Every Day Better *Than Before and instruct them to complete Week 1 before your next group meeting.*

*5. Gather and distribute contact information for the group.*

*6. Pray that God will make you stronger in Him. Consider having prayer partners for the duration of the study.*

## SESSION 2

Preview the video session. Welcome group members and pray. Begin either by inviting group members to share some of the responses to their study this week or by viewing the video. Then, as time permits, discuss some of the following questions from the first week's study.

*1. What were some of the reasons you "can't commit" to the next 40 days (p. 11)?*

*2. Based on what you already know, list some of the immediate things that change when someone believes Jesus (p. 17).*

*3. How have you seen someone being changed as he or she continued to follow Jesus (p. 17)?*

*4. What did you jot down as ways you have felt in over your spiritual head (p. 21)?*

*5. What were some of the ways you listed about how we should value and respect the image-bearing of all human beings (p. 26)?*

*6. How did your first 5 of the 40 days go? Did you glean any new truths or notice something in the first 12 chapters of Psalms that you hadn't before?*

## SESSION 3

Preview the video in preparation for the session. Welcome group members and pray. Begin either by inviting group members to share some of the responses to their study this week or by viewing the video. Then, as time permits, discuss some of the following questions from the second week's study.

*1. What were some of your questions you listed on page 35? How has this week's personal study helped answer any of those questions?*

*2. When God graciously reveals to us an area of compromise, how should we respond (p. 38)?*

*3. Sometimes people do not respond quickly to a revealed area of disobedience or compromise. Why do you think that happens (p. 38)?*

*4. Share any places in your life where God has been asking you to obey Him by faith (p. 38).*

*5. When you consider sin of pride in your own life, do you see places where your pride became a wrecking ball of pain and destruction (p. 42)?*

*6. As you think about the people in your own life, what characteristics do you see in the people who live without God (p. 53)?*

*7. What reasons do you hear other people give when they refuse to believe or accept the love of God?*

*8. Share some of the blessings from God that you've experienced through your own suffering (p. 60).*

## SESSION 4

Welcome group members and pray. Begin either by inviting group members to share some of the responses to their study this week or by viewing the video. Then, as time permits, discuss some of the following questions from the third week's study.

*1. What would you say is the most common personal struggle affecting women in our culture (p. 70)?*

*2. What were some of the ways you listed on page 71 that insecurity affects our lives?*

*3. How did you respond to the question on page 73: How would you respond if God asked you to teach someone else what you've been learning about Him?*

*4. We learned a lot about the law this week (Day 14). Did you learn anything new? Explain.*

5. What about some of the Bible words we studied this week? Have you heard them before? How do you have a better understanding of these theological words (pp. 81-83)?

6. Do you agree with Tim Keller's statement on page 91: "It's impossible to meet the real Jesus and leave indifferent"? Why or why not?

## SESSION 5
Welcome group members and pray. Begin either by inviting group members to share some of the responses to their study this week or by viewing the video. Then, as time permits, discuss some of the following questions from the fourth week's study.

1. Share your redeemed story using the questions on page 100.

2. Have you ever struggled with the "doing" of worship? Explain (p. 103).

3. How do you respond to the following statement: "When you are redeemed, your relationship with God has changed. Your life and mission here on earth have changed. Your future life in eternity has changed" (p. 107)?

4. When you meet a woman who knows she's forgiven, what is the most noticeable thing about her? How does someone live like she's forgiven (p. 113)?

5. Do you ever feel like this world is not your home? Like you're not there yet? When have you felt that way recently (p. 115)?

6. What are the top three areas of your life where it's time to declare God's peace (not chaos) belongs to you (p. 116)?

7. Share some of your "assignments" from the activity on page 118.

## SESSION 6
Welcome group members and pray. Begin either by inviting group members to share some of the responses to their study this week or by viewing the video. Then, as time permits, discuss some of the following questions from the fifth week's study.

1. When you think about your spiritual growth, have there been times you grew more than others? Times you went backward instead of forward (p. 127)? Explain.

2. Share some of the struggles you're facing from the activity on page 130.

3. When you look back at Keller's definitions of idolatry, how are you convicted in your own heart (p. 136)?

4. Discuss some of the good things that we allow to become god-things in our lives (p. 142).

5. Do you recognize places in your own life where you only felt a worldly grief so you continued to repeat the same sin patterns with the same consequences over and over? Explain (p. 146).

6. Share any uncovered idols that you feel comfortable sharing with your group (p. 148).

## SESSION 7

Welcome group members and pray. Begin either by inviting group members to share some of the responses to their study this week or by viewing the video. Then, as time permits, discuss some of the following questions from the final week's study.

1. *Why do you think it's hard for most of us to grow in our faith? To let God change our lives (p. 154)?*

2. *Do you forget how much God has blessed you? What makes you forget (p. 155)?*

3. *Share some of the ways you remind yourself not to forget (p. 155).*

4. *How are you seeing your character being redeemed (p. 163)?*

5. *Describe the person who lives with a constant FOMO (p. 170).*

6. *Now, describe the person who lives assured that God's eternity includes all (p. 170).*

7. *What ways do you see the fear of man manifest in life (p. 171)?*

# 40 DAYS: THE PSALMS, MEDITATION, AND PRAYER

Why in the world did I add 40 days of Psalms, meditation, and prayer to this study? Well, you can thank my small group of squirrelly, middle school girls from Arlington, Texas, for all this. Amy, Missy, Erin, Christy, Kenalea, Cheryl, Julie, Carmen, Sheralyn, Cathy, Kim, Sarah, Leslie, and Mary are all grown up now. They've become beautiful wives, moms, and friends, but none of them will let me forget the summer I tried to teach them how to pray.

I was the seminary intern that summer at Pantego Bible Church. They were the silly, joy-filled girls who stole my heart and agreed to meet with me once a week for the summer. I can't remember one thing we talked about, but I do know I wanted to challenge them to grow in prayer. So I did the only creative thing I could think of and brought a kitchen timer every week. We were going to pray until the timer went off.

Our first week of prayer time went pretty well. The timer went off at five minutes, and the girls high-fived one another like old prayer warriors. Every week after, I added five more minutes to the timer, and they'd whine like little babies. But by the end of the summer, we were up to 45

minutes of prayer and those precious girls knew a couple of things for sure. They could pray longer than they ever believed they could. And, there is a lot to pray about when you finally stop and start to pray.

During our 40 days of prayer, our family read *Draw the Circle* by pastor Mark Batterson. He says, "If you want God to do something new in your life, you can't do the same old thing."[1]

One thing is certain, 40 days will definitely help kick start a new prayer life and maybe even begin a new prayer habit in your life!

## SOME PRACTICAL THOUGHTS FOR ACTUALLY PRAYING

To shake up our routine and jog ourselves into better listening, Scott and I began our 40 days of prayer with empty prayer journals. We were also reading other books on prayer, both old and new, and listening to sermon podcasts about prayer. We just wanted to increase our prayer focus and the power of our prayers.

Scott and I usually prayed separately in the mornings. He has a prayer chair. I'm usually on the floor in my home office, sometimes laying prostrate, sometimes sitting, sometimes pacing, and lots of times going back and forth between all those. I have prayed on the floor of my walk-in closet, underneath the baby bed, or sitting in the parking lot of the grocery store, just to have a quiet place. Years before the *War Room* movie, my girlfriend built a house with a prayer closet underneath the stairs in the center of her house. It was a perfect, small space, cozy but not distracting. She had a lamp, bulletin board, paper, pens, a Bible, but not much else. It wasn't a reading room. It was a prayer room. The kids left prayer requests in there for her to find. I thought it was the most brilliant idea I'd ever heard of.

Most of the time, I am praying all throughout the day for anything that comes to mind or requests I've committed to pray for. Many of you probably do the same thing. First Thessalonians 5:17 calls us to "pray without ceasing." But I hope your prayer time these 40 days can become an actual, set-apart time that eventually becomes your regular, daily prayer.

Some people do better praying with friends because accountability helps the praying to actually happen. Some of my friends pray together each day on the phone. Some walk together and pray as they walk. Are you getting the idea, that the most important thing is actually praying, no matter how or where it happens!

### MEDITATION

As we're reading through the Book of Psalms together, I hope you learn to sit quietly for a moment to think about what you've read and how God might be speaking directly to you. Consider how the words you read might apply to your life or a situation you are facing. That is meditation. Right now, our culture thinks meditation is cool, but what they promote isn't biblical meditation. Cultural meditation, or mindfulness, is about turning your focus inward. Biblical meditation turns our focus God-ward. It's a totally different

thing. There is nothing inside of me that can give me peace. Peace is a gift from God that grows in the soul being redeemed.

We prayerfully meditate in God's presence as we transition from study to prayer because we're entering a conversation God began in His Word. We respond with meditation, listening, and prayer.

### READING THROUGH THE BOOK OF PSALMS

To meditate on a particular passage in Psalms, read through the words, meditate on their meaning, make some notes if you want to, then personalize those words and pray them back to God. For instance,

One generation shall
commend your works
to another, and shall
declare your mighty acts.
On the glorious splendor
of your majesty, and on
your wondrous works,
I will meditate.
PSALM 145:4-5

*Father, teach me to meditate on Your majesty. Teach me how to meditate on Your glory. Show me how to commend Your glory to the next generation. I want to learn to declare Your mighty acts in ways they can hear.*

### THE BIBLE YOU READ

There are lots of mobile versions of the Bible you can download for free. So, I hope you have a Bible on everything you own! Lisa Harper says she plays the audio Bible in her house all through the night, so the Word is continually being spoken over them. Brilliant. Another friend, Amy Heywood, plays the audio Bible in the mornings as she drives the kids to school. They are all kind of sleepy, so it's a good listening time.

As awesome as technology is, I do hope you have a physical, hold-in-your-hand Bible of your own. You can Google "free Bible" to find several organizations who will be glad to send you a Bible of your own. This past weekend, my son zipped up my Bible in the front pocket of my roller bag, and I spent 24 hours thinking it might be gone. When he remembered where it was, it was happy dance all around! My little notes in the margins. My underlines. My dates and circled words. I hope you have a precious copy of God's Word.

## BEGINNING WITH THE LORD'S PRAYER

Actually beginning to pray may be your hardest thing. That's why I usually lay down on the floor somewhere in my house, or on towels at the hotel. I'm not sure why that physical act instantly focuses my head, but it does. And then there are the words. How do we begin talking to God? Sometimes words begin before I can lay down, and sometimes they don't. Timothy Keller wrote about beginning our prayer time by making the Lord's Prayer our personal prayer. Many days, that's exactly how I begin.

When I begin with the Lord's Prayer, I am beginning with God and His glory, not me and my needs. It's amazing how intentional we have to be to center our thoughts on Him first.

## THE PRAYER REQUESTS

Scott and I both used little blank journals to make notes about our prayers, but I'm now trying index cards to see if that's a better system

for me. Paul Miller, author of *A Praying Life*, uses one card for each person or organization, etc.[2] I now have cards with the kids' names written at the top, then I write the ways I am led to pray for each one, a verse I am praying, answers, and so forth. My friend has a big chalkboard painted wall where her family writes prayer requests. There's probably even a Pinterest board with a thousand cool ways to organize your prayer requests!

In my personal prayer time, I keep my journal or cards beside me, writing down anything God prompts me to "circle" in prayer. Sometimes I write the date of something specific or an answer to prayer that has come.

Beginning our 40 days with an empty prayer journal was kind of intimidating, but Scott and I later realized that we grew so much as we learned to wait and listen for God's prompting. It was almost like we were leaning into God as hard as we could, straining to hear His voice. Honestly, I didn't write very much in my journal the first few days. I think it took awhile to re-learn how to quiet my soul, instead of jumping into an already prepared "list."

## ONE LAST THOUGHT

Some days you will be a prayer warrior. Other days you will be pitiful. The power has never been in your prayers. The power to redeem your life fully resides in the One to whom you pray.

Just. Keep. Praying.

1. Mark Batterson, *Draw The Circle, The 40 Day Prayer Challenge* (Grand Rapids, MI: Zondervan, 2012), 7-8.

2. Paul Miller, *A Praying Life, Connecting with God in a Distracting World* (Colorado Springs, CO: Navpress, 2009), 235-238.

# Also from Angela Thomas-Pharr

## STRONGER:
### Finding Hope in Fragile Places
7 sessions

God is stronger than every struggle you will ever face. End the self-focused distractions of striving, comparison, and performance by living a confident, transformed, Christ-radiating life marked by His strength.

**Bible Study Book**
005513458     *$12.99*
**Leader Kit**
005474740     *$149.99*

## BRAVE:
### Honest Questions Women Ask
7 sessions

We've all got insecurities, flaws, and struggles we're afraid to address. But if we can be brave enough to raise the questions, God will answer us.

**Bible Study Book**
005342722     *$12.99*
**Leader Kit**
005342721     *$149.99*